LEAD TO SUCCEED

NEW TESTAMENT PRINCIPLES FOR VISIONARY LEADERSHIP

STAN TOLER & JERRY BRECHEISEN

Beacon Hill Press of Kansas City
Kansas City, Missouri

Copyright 2003
by Beacon Hill Press of Kansas City

ISBN 083-411-9803

Printed in the
United States of America

All Scripture quotations not otherwise designated are from the *Holy Bible, New International Version*® (NIV®). Copyright © 1973, 1978, 1984 by International Bible Society. Used by permission of Zondervan Publishing House. All rights reserved.

Permission to quote from the following additional copyrighted versions of the Bible is acknowledged with appreciation:

The *Holy Bible, New Living Translation* (NLT), copyright © 1996. Used by permission of Tyndale House Publishers, Inc., Wheaton, IL 60189. All rights reserved.

The Message (TM). Copyright © 1993, 1994, 1995, 1996, 2000, 2001, 2002. Used by permission of NavPress Publishing Group.

Scripture quotations marked KJV are from the King James Version.

Library of Congress Cataloging-in-Publication Data

Toler, Stan.
   Lead to succeed : New Testament principles for visionary leadership / Stan Toler, Jerry Brecheisen.
     p. cm.
Includes bibliographical references.
   ISBN 0-8341-1980-3 (pbk.)
   1. Christian leadership. 2. Christian leadership—Biblical teaching. 3. Bible. N.T.—Criticism, interpretation, etc. I. Brecheisen, Jerry. II. Title.

   BV652.1.T645 2003
   253—dc21

                                                            2003011066

10   9   8   7   6   5   4   3   2   1

To
Bill and Jan Burch.
Thanks for your godly leadership
and influence on my life.
—Stan Toler

To
Dr. Thomas E. and Joan Phillippe,
whose leadership and friendship
have been a continual source of inspiration.
—Jerry Brecheisen

ABOUT THE AUTHORS

Stan Toler is senior pastor of Trinity Church of the Nazarene in Oklahoma City. For several years he taught seminars for INJOY Group, a leadership development institute. Stan has written over 45 books, including his best-sellers *God Has Never Failed Me, but He's Sure Scared Me to Death a Few Times* and *The Five-Star Church.*

For additional information on seminars, scheduling speaking engagements, or to contact the author:

Stan Toler
P.O. Box 892170
Oklahoma City, OK 73189-2170
E-mail: stoler1107@aol.com
Web site: www.stantoler.com

Jerry Brecheisen (pronounced "breck-eye-zen") has spent nearly his entire life in music, speaking, and media ministries. Currently the managing editor of his denomination's magazine and producer of its international radio ministry, he traveled over 15 years in his family's gospel music ministry and served 28 years in pastoral ministry—22 years as senior pastor in multiple staff churches.

He has authored 11 books personally and has coauthored, edited, or compiled over 20 books for major publishers and well-known Christian personalities. He is a magazine columnist, has written numerous articles for Christian magazines, and regularly contributes to on-line magazines.

Jerry and his wife, Carol, reside in Indianapolis. They have two married children, Mandi Cundiff and Arianna Eckart, and are the proud grandparents of three.

For additional information on seminars, scheduling, speaking engagements, or to contact the author:

Jerry Brecheisen
P.O. Box 6073
Fishers, IN 46038
E-mail: jerry@brecksong.com
Web site: www.brecksong.com

CONTENTS

ACKNOWLEDGMENTS

Special thanks to Bonnie Perry, Hardy Weathers, Jonathan Wright, Deloris Leonard, and Pat Diamond.

—Stan Toler

Special thanks to my wife, Carol, for her editorial skill and faithful assistance.

Special thanks also to Lawrence Wilson for assisting with the research and for providing editorial insight.

—Jerry Brecheisen

INTRODUCTION

A little boy excitedly reported his day at kindergarten. "Mom, guess what—I learned my numbers today!" he announced.

"That's great!" his proud mom responded. "What are you going to do with all that learning?"

"Well, Mom," he answered, "the next time we go on a vacation trip, I'll tell you the 'how far.'" Then he added, "But somebody's still gonna have to help me with the 'where to'!"

Columnist Michael B. Ross said, "The roles of religious leadership are changing so rapidly that communities of faith are unable to keep up. The results? Disillusioned and marginalized clergy leading discouraged, unfocused congregations."[1] Obviously, we know the "how-fars," but we still need someone who will be willing to point out the "where-tos."

As usual, God's Word fills in the gaps. From John the Baptist to John the Revelator, the New Testament gives practical examples of godly leadership to help us with our "where-tos." Thoroughly dedicated men and women in the Early Church fought the godless tides of their times and effectively led people to a greater understanding of God and of their own God-given potential.

An Associated Press article told of a freight train that traveled 70 miles by itself. Forty-seven cars attached to a diesel engine traveled along an Ohio railroad track at speeds of nearly 50 miles per hour without a single rider on board. And to make matters worse, the train was carrying hazardous materials. For some unknown reason, as it was being assembled it suddenly took off under its own power. Police and railroad personnel scrambled to clear railroad crossings as the train moved through surprised cities and towns. Finally a railroad employee jogged alongside the runaway train, grabbed a railing on the engine, and hoisted himself on board, bringing an end to the train's unscheduled journey.

There are times when leading people is like trying to stop a runaway train. They're moving under their own power toward a self-serving and potentially dangerous destination faster than a freshman saying grace in a high school cafeteria, while the leader-engineer simply jogs alongside, frustrated and often out of breath.

At other times, "all the king's horses and all the king's men" can't get the train to leave the station. The machinery may be in place, the tracks may be set, and the route may be planned—but the train won't budge.

The heart of this book is to show you how to apply the actions and attitudes of outstanding New Testament leaders to move the train forward.

Leith Anderson wrote, "Leadership has always been difficult. It was hard for Moses, David, Paul, Martin Luther, and Abraham Lincoln. Are some leadership positions more difficult than others? Of course. Is leadership more difficult now than it used to be? In many ways, yes."[2]

Most modern leaders would agree. The carpet in your office probably has a few blood, sweat, and tear stains that prove the point.

Lead to Succeed: New Testament Principles for Visionary Leadership is for leaders in times like these—times when motivating people to goodness or good works is about as easy as trying to put a dinosaur into the passenger compartment of a Dodge truck.

It's not about *methods,* however. Though leadership methods are seen throughout, this book is about motivations, about the very character qualities that make a vibrant leader.

It's for the leader who finds himself or herself standing alongside the Old Testament prophet Isaiah as he reads the indictment against a spiritually stubborn society and then realizes that he himself has a few personal challenges of his own. Suddenly Isaiah's pronouncement of "woe" against the sins and stupidity of Judah (Isa. 5) is seen in the light of his own shortcomings, especially when he gets a glimpse of the perfection of the Almighty: "'Woe to me!' I cried. 'I am ruined! For I am a man of unclean lips, and I live among a people of unclean lips, and my eyes have seen the King, the LORD Almighty'" (6:5).

Before he lobs another eighth-century "woe" on the masses, he hunkers down in the bunker of his heart and takes a personal, spiritual inventory. He asks, "What adjustments can I make in my own life that will positively affect the lives of others?"

Most often people won't follow a leader who isn't leading. People usually follow those who practice their own principles. The apostle Paul had a handle on that when he wrote to the Corinthians,

> Even though you have ten thousand guardians in Christ, you do not have many fathers, for in Christ Jesus I became your father through the gospel. Therefore I urge you to imitate me. For this reason I am sending to you Timothy, my son whom I love, who is faithful in the Lord. He will remind you of my way of life in Christ Jesus, which agrees with what I teach everywhere in every church *(1 Cor. 4:15-17)*.

The chain of leadership in Paul's ministry began with a strong link: his own life of faith in Christ. Thomas Watson said, "Nothing so conclusively proves a man's ability to lead others as what he does from day to day to lead himself."

So vibrant Christian leadership begins with a vibrant Christian. Those who are moving forward in their own faith and personal growth are those who are most apt to lead others.

Several New Testament leaders give us the best leadership illustration. As they struggled to keep the Church's head above the raging waters of their time, they preached, taught, and organized powerfully and productively.

We pray that your own leadership will be rejuvenated by their wonderful example. And we pray that God will use this book to help you lead people forward, even when they're standing still.

In this book, you will

- learn 10 principles for vibrant leadership.
- discover practical methods of leadership from New Testament leaders.
- understand the importance of integrating personal faith with public leadership.
- recognize leadership characteristics essential for moving people forward.
- learn how to utilize your energy for maximum effectiveness.
- grasp tools for dealing with personal or corporate adversity.
- find new ways to deal with people in a manner that reflects your faith in Christ.

You'll also discover that a bit of humor applied to the haunting tasks of leadership helps rather than hurts. The authors realize that the subject of leadership can be as serious as the times, but we pledge to construct a few "benches" along the journey, where you can sit a spell and be refreshed with the hilarious promises of God in the midst of life's predicaments.

Our insights are neither new nor final. But you can be assured that they have been forged in the fires of frontline leadership, not only over our cumulative span of 70 years of personal ministry but more importantly in the lives of New Testament leaders who have grasped the power and promises of an eternal God.

This book will always be a work in progress. But we hope these first steps will be a great help to you in your own journey.

During a rousing political speech against all the evils of society, a speaker threw down the gauntlet and announced, "I pledge to do my best to rid the world of communism, socialism, and anarchism."

A slight pause followed as the orator tried to catch his breath.

An elderly man on the front row rose slowly and pointed a shaking cane toward the podium. "And if you need any help, you can count on me," he said enthusiastically. "I've been fightin' to get rid of rheumatism for the last 10 years!"

We all need help as we face the seemingly unfinished tasks and unfaithful volunteers who so characterize this new millennium. It's our prayer that this book will be just the kind of help and encouragement you need.

1 Making Christ Your Pattern

A HISTORY PROFESSOR COMMENTED on Christopher Columbus's discovery of America, saying that there were three significant aspects of the trip. One, before he left, he didn't have a clue as to where he was going. Two, when he arrived, he didn't have a clue as to where he was. And three, when he got ready to leave, he didn't have a clue as to how to get back home.

From the back of the room a history major spoke up: "And four, he didn't have a clue as to how he was ever going to pay back that loan to the government!"

Thankfully, when it comes to Christian leadership, we can be a little more informed. We have the greatest leadership model.

The Lord Jesus Christ is God's final word on leadership.

He is the divine *Logos*. God the Father communicated leadership principles through His Son. Earth's greatest Leader was born on the wrong side of the tracks. He had no earthly office space—in fact, the birds of the air had better accommodations—and He never had an expense account. He didn't have an MBA from an Ivy League college, and *Fortune* magazine never featured Him. Nevertheless, He put His Creator skill on a self-sacrificing shelf and humbly learned to be an earthly leader at the side of a Nazareth carpenter's bench.

At His Jordan River baptism, God announced His approval of Him, and the Holy Spirit descended in power upon His human frame.

From there, Jesus of Nazareth led a few rough souls from the attics of obscurity to the pinnacles of Christian history. His God-blessed leadership mixed compassion with iron-willed tenacity. His words angered some and caused others to weep.

He encouraged. He chastised. He forgave. He spoke with authority and lived with authenticity. He never gave up on those whom He led—even if it meant His own death. Every leader would be wise to *learn* from Him, *live* like Him, and *follow* His leadership principles.

11

Whether you're leading by accident or by appointment, there's hope in following the Master. Along with His disciples, He pounded some direction signs into the soil of their times that will help us in our journey.

THE GREAT PREREQUISITE FOR CHRISTIAN LEADERSHIP

The New Testament is a survival manual for people in the trenches of leadership.

One of the most influential leaders in the New Testament was John the Baptist. Crowds of people pushed and shoved to hear the words of this straight-talking messenger of the Messiah who wore designer suits made of camel hair.

But what was the root of that influence? According to John 1:23, when the religious leaders asked for his credentials, "John replied in the words of Isaiah the prophet, 'I am the voice of one calling in the desert, "Make straight the way for the Lord."'"

John the Baptist knew who he was. He had heavenly connections. His leadership strengths didn't come from books or seminars, conferences or conventions. As vital as those edge-sharpening tools may be, John's greatest leadership strengths came from the power and promises focused on and flowing from the Messiah. And his message to the masses about the Christ was always the same: "He must become greater; I must become less" (John 3:30).

Our real power for leadership is in our connection to heaven—in surrendering to and gaining strength from the power of a risen Christ. That's seen in these powerful words of His:

> I am the true vine, and my Father is the gardener. He cuts off every branch in me that bears no fruit, while every branch that does bear fruit he prunes so that it will be even more fruitful. You are already clean because of the word I have spoken to you. Remain in me, and I will remain in you. No branch can bear fruit by itself; it must remain in the vine. Neither can you bear fruit unless you remain in me. I am the vine; you are the branches. If a man remains in me and I in him, he will bear much fruit; apart from me you can do nothing (John 15:1-5).

The scores of laypersons that have been trained in the evangelism and discipleship methods of Campus Crusade for Christ International have heard that scriptural mandate over and over: "Apart from me you can do nothing."

Faith in Christ is the channel of spiritual life for leaders!

A Christian leader will never lead people forward for Christ without first taking his or her own trip to the Cross. Without the electricity of Calvary's flow, human leaders are powerless.

Twentieth-century songwriter Jessie B. Pounds said it well:

I must needs go home by the way of the cross;

There's no other way but this.

I shall ne'er get sight of the Gates of Light

If the way of the cross I miss.

There is no bypass. Anyone who would seek to influence others for Christ must take a direct route to the Cross. A personal faith in the Lord Jesus Christ (John 1:12) is the great prerequisite for Christian leadership.

Make Sure the Captain Is at the Controls

During a commuter flight the plane seemed to bounce excessively. Wanting to soothe the nerves of the concerned passengers, the pilot walked from the cockpit and stood in the aisle to make an announcement: "Ladies and gentlemen, there's nothing to worry about. We're just having a little problem with engine number two. In fact, I'll be honest with you—the engine has quit running. But you'll be glad to know that we have three other engines that are working properly."

Walking toward the cockpit, the pilot suddenly turned around and said, "Oh, I almost forgot. You'll also be relieved to know that we have three pastors on board this flight."

Loud enough for everyone in the tiny commuter plane to hear, the passenger in the front row turned to his seatmate and said, "I don't know about you, but I'd just as soon have four good engines!"

Even with four good engines, some flights are bouncy and unpredictable. Sometimes there are weather delays that affect the arrival. Sometimes there are miscalculations about fuel supply. Sometimes there's simply too much baggage on board.

But whatever the problem may be, you can be assured that the final responsibility is the captain's. Without his or her control, the whole flight is somewhat endangered.

It may be elementary, but it's a vital lesson on leadership. All the engines of organizational programs, property, or personnel are ultimately endangered unless the Captain, Christ, is at the controls. "Apart from me you can do nothing" (John 15:5).

So Christian leadership begins with an evaluation of its dependence on the Captain. "Search me, O God, and know my heart" (Ps. 139:23). Until the *heart* of the leader is right before God, the *works* of the leader will ultimately be ineffective.

God calls the leader to a quiet place—away from the noise of nonessentials—and invites him or her to look over the spiritual checklist. Here are some items that might be on it:

- "Is Christ the Lord of my life?"
- "Am I trying to operate on His strength or my own?"
- "Do I consistently seek the wisdom of His Word?"
- "Do I talk to Him in prayer before I talk to the people?"
- "Am I relying on the power of His Holy Spirit?"
- "Are there hidden things in my life that I need to confess to Him?"
- "Am I in fellowship with His people?"
- "Is He first in my planning process?"
- "Do my programs and methods honor Him?"

Hudson T. Armerding, former president of Wheaton College, wrote, "The Christian leader must determine that he will go God's way and not make his decisions on the basis of such considerations as his relationship with the hierarchy, or his financial reward, or his status. Furthermore, he must be spiritually discerning in his willingness to identify himself with the people of God."[1]

God's way.

God's people.

Sounds a lot like Christian leadership—the kind of leadership intent on moving people forward when they're standing still!

FOLLOW THE LEADER'S LEADERSHIP

God's word on leadership is seen in the practices and priorities of Jesus Christ. The disciplines and patterns of His life affected His leadership. His character traits modeled the best of Christian leadership. And His absolute sincerity set the course for His earthly ministry.

1. Jesus was sincere in His purpose

Jesus of Nazareth had divine direction. He was always aware of a higher purpose, always moving toward Calvary. The Master was on a monumental mission to buy back the souls claimed by Satan in Eden's yard sale.

"The Son of Man came to seek and to save what was lost" (Luke 19:10).

So everything He did in that tiny window of time on earth (three short years) moved Him toward fulfilling His calling.

Even as a child, He had a sense of duty that loomed above the daily regimens of His life. During the Feast of the Passover celebration in Jerusalem, a 12-year-old Jesus became separated from His parents. Upon finding Him in the Temple among religious leaders and teachers, Jesus' parents corrected Him for wandering away. But He had wandered only from their watchful eye—not from the way, not from the path that His Heavenly Father had carved out of the forests of time. He replied to Mary and Joseph, "Why were you searching for me? . . . Didn't you know I had to be in my Father's house?" (Luke 2:49). He was where He belonged, doing what He was born to do—ministering to people.

There was an absolute purity in Jesus' purpose. Above all, He sincerely sought His Father's will for the redemption of humanity. "Not my will, but yours be done" (Luke 22:42).

In the classic Sherlock Holmes whodunit novel *Scandal in Bohemia,* Watson is pressed into service to witness the marriage of the protagonist. In a typically twisted turn of events, the newly married couple drives off from the cathedral site of their marriage of convenience in different carriages. Watson's observations of the events surprisingly describe many organizations—Christian or otherwise— "They drove away in different directions, and I went off to make my own arrangements."

Christian leadership without direction or purpose is dangerous at best. Many "gospel ships" have wrecked on the rocks of time because some sailor neglected to set the sails properly.

Christlike leadership always focuses on the main thing.

What is it? *Redemption.*

Jesus spelled it out for us in His prayer to the Father for His disciples, "As you sent me into the world, I have sent them into the world" (John 17:18).

Every Christian leader already has a direction, a purpose: to bring people to the Kingdom, to a personal and vital faith in the Lord Jesus Christ. That's the bottom line—now and forever.

Everything else is incidental. Packing people into pews or adding step stools on organizational flowcharts isn't what it's all about.

There's no better job description than that found in the Great Commission (Matt. 28:18-20).

Direction is of utmost importance. There is a dynamic in a destination.

When we leave our home and go out the front door, we don't usually announce to our friends or loved ones, "I'm going anywhere—be back sometime!"

Our direction is usually a bit more specific. We start out for "somewhere," not "anywhere." "Somewhere" has a cohesive direction to it—a certain place, an estimated arrival, a prescribed route. "Anywhere" is confusing, aimless, and haphazard.

It's said that professional ice hockey great Wayne Gretzky "was better at the game of hockey, perhaps, than anyone ever because he knew where the puck was going, not just where it had been. Turn out the lights in the middle of a play, his coach said, and Gretzky would still know where every player was on the ice."[2]

People who are "standing still" obviously lack direction. They are "anywhere" folks rather than "somewhere" folks. They are happy with the haphazard and content with the confusing. In a "revised version" of the well-known gospel song, they seem to be "leaning on the everlasting *charms.*" They are deceptively charmed by their inertia, mesmerized by their motionlessness. They like *who* they are, *what* they are, and *where* they are well enough not to bother moving.

If you would be a leader who moves people forward, you'll need a sincere purpose. You'll need to understand exactly *why* you're doing *what* you're intending to do. And then you'll bravely move in that direction.

The sheer synergy of direction is bound to set a few tennis shoes or wing tips in motion!

Redemption was of ultimate importance to the Lord Jesus Christ. Every event in the busyness of Jesus' day was a redemptive act.

Every earthly activity had the ultimate end of sacrifice and surrender to fulfill the higher purpose of bringing people to the Kingdom. "As the time approached for him to be taken up to heaven, Jesus resolutely set out for Jerusalem" (Luke 9:51).

There was a hidden agenda in His every act of leadership; there was a "Cross reference" in everything.

What's your purpose?

- To further the kingdom of God *or* to gain personal recognition?
- To establish Christians in their faith *or* to gather loyalty to yourself?
- To build up the church of Christ *or* to build a personal kingdom?

Which of your objectives need to be discarded? Which need to be developed?

Christlike leadership is more than leading people from Point A to Point B. It's more than working through some corporate "to do" list. It's a commitment of the heart to offer oneself to help others become everything that God intended.

The wedding ceremony had reached the moment of lighting the unity candle. The bride and groom moved from the altar up to the candle on the platform.

The pastor whispered instructions to the couple just to make sure they remembered what to do: "Each of you take the candles on the outside, light the center candle together, and then blow out your individual candles."

The pastor then explained to the audience that the blowing out of the two outer candles represented the couple's surrender of their individual freedom.

The groom suddenly thought about the significance of the act and whispered back to the pastor, "Would it be all right if we just blow out her candle?"

Obviously the apostle Paul had blown his candle out. He had a strong sense of purpose that found its fulfillment in surrendering to Christ:

> Whatever was to my profit I now consider loss for the sake of Christ. What is more, I consider everything a loss compared to the surpassing greatness of knowing Christ Jesus my Lord, for

whose sake I have lost all things. I consider them rubbish, that I may gain Christ and be found in him, not having a righteousness of my own that comes from the law, but that which is through faith in Christ—the righteousness that comes from God and is by faith. I want to know Christ and the power of his resurrection and the fellowship of sharing in his sufferings, becoming like him in his death, and so, somehow, to attain to the resurrection from the dead.

Not that I have already obtained all this, or have already been made perfect, but I press on to take hold of that for which Christ Jesus took hold of me. Brothers, I do not consider myself yet to have taken hold of it. But one thing I do: Forgetting what is behind and straining toward what is ahead, I press on toward the goal to win the prize for which God has called me heavenward in Christ Jesus (Phil. 3:7-14).

2. Jesus was sincere in His service to others

It was just before the Passover Feast. Jesus knew that the time had come for him to leave this world and go to the Father. Having loved his own who were in the world, he now showed them the full extent of his love.

The evening meal was being served, and the devil had already prompted Judas Iscariot, son of Simon, to betray Jesus. Jesus knew that the Father had put all things under his power, and that he had come from God and was returning to God; so he got up from the meal, took off his outer clothing, and wrapped a towel around his waist. After that, he poured water into a basin and began to wash his disciples' feet, drying them with the towel that was wrapped around him.

He came to Simon Peter, who said to him, "Lord, are you going to wash my feet?"

Jesus replied, "You do not realize now what I am doing, but later you will understand."

"No," said Peter, "you shall never wash my feet."

Jesus answered, "Unless I wash you, you have no part with me."

"Then, Lord," Simon Peter replied, "not just my feet but my hands and my head as well!"

Jesus answered, "A person who has had a bath needs only to wash his feet; his whole body is clean. And you are clean, though not every one of you." For he knew who was going to betray him, and that was why he said not every one was clean.

When he had finished washing their feet, he put on his clothes and returned to his place. "Do you understand what I have done for you?" he asked them. "You call me 'Teacher' and 'Lord,' and rightly so, for that is what I am. Now that I, your Lord and Teacher, have washed your feet, you also should wash one another's feet. I have set you an example that you should do as I have done for you" *(John 13:1-15)*.

If you're looking for a leadership model, you've found it. Jesus of Nazareth should have been on the receiving end of that foot washing! Everything that exists came from His hand. He owns the stars. He planted every blade of grass. He applied the golden hue to every field flower. He pointed the rays of the sun to a million darkened valleys. He deserved to be treated like royalty. Instead, He grabbed a towel and taught some astonished disciples how to motivate others by loving and serving them.

Understand the significance of service. God-inspired, Spirit-empowered, loving service is one of the great motivators.

A family with fussy kids had been traveling all day in a sport utility vehicle.

The father's dour face told its own story as he dutifully went into a seafood restaurant and asked the waitress, "Lady, do you serve crabs here?"

She took one look at the grumpy traveler and quickly responded, "Sure! We'll serve anyone. Have a seat, and I'll be right with you!"

Vibrant leadership looks to the grateful or the grumpy and says, "Have a seat, and I'll be right with you."

Granted, many times the Christian leader feels more like wielding a stick rather than a towel! The stubbornness, childishness, carnality, and lethargy of others are characteristics that haunt the leader and hinder progress.

Jesus was not immune to such behavior. The New Testament pathways were crowded with careless, crude, or crummy pedestrians. Even His disciples had their pouting spells, attention-grabbings, get-ahead aches, and spiritual mob rule.

Someone once said, "Every group has at least one difficult person in it. If you don't immediately recognize who that person is—it's probably you!"

Just like any leader, Jesus faced the disappointments of working with people who failed to live up to their potential, who didn't keep their promises, who put themselves first over the greater cause.

Even His closest associates misunderstood His calling. For example, when Jesus talked about a "kingdom," His disciples were thinking about an earthly "democracy" instead of a heavenly "theocracy."

You'll remember that at the glorious moment of His transfiguration, His inner circle of disciples tried to turn its beauty into a building program!

> After six days Jesus took Peter, James and John with him and led them up a high mountain, where they were all alone. There he was transfigured before them. His clothes became dazzling white, whiter than anyone in the world could bleach them. And there appeared before them Elijah and Moses, who were talking with Jesus. Peter said to Jesus, "Rabbi, it is good for us to be here. Let us put up three shelters—one for you, one for Moses and one for Elijah" (Mark 9:2-5).

It was the same bunch that tried to stop Jesus from washing their feet and thereby expressing His love and duty to them. Instead of handing out layoff notices, Jesus chose to extend a towel. Instead of berating, He chose a blessing. And the hearts of His followers melted like a snow cone under an Oklahoma summer sun.

Jesus always looked beyond the imperfections of His colleagues to their potential. He taught us the advantages of acceptance, the incentive of kindness, and the lasting influence of sincere love and service.

- He always accepted people as they were and helped them become better.
- He understood that God-given abilities are stored in jars of clay.
- He focused on restoration and healing, bringing honor out of the flaws.

One of the great love stories in history is that of Winston Churchill and his beloved wife, Clemmie. Biographer James C. Humes gives a vivid example: "At a very formal gathering, Churchill was asked, 'If you could not be who you are, who would you like to be?' Churchill responded, 'If I could not be who I am, I would most like to be'—and here he paused to take his wife's hand—'Lady Churchill's second husband.'"[3]

As an honored guest in the midst of an elaborate ceremony, the great leader chose to focus on the person whom he loved. Most everything else that happened on that occasion has been forgotten, but the devotion of a husband to his wife has lived on.

You'll never rise so high as when you stoop to give honor and service to another. In PreachingToday.com Madeleine L'Engle was quoted: "Following Christ has nothing to do with success as the world sees success. It has to do with love."[4]

John the Baptist said, "He must become greater; I must become less" (John 3:30). And the influence that matters is His love and presence working its wonderful way through the actions and attitudes of the Christian leader.

3. Jesus was sincere in His communications

Leith Anderson said, "Leadership is about leaders, followers, organizations, circumstances, power, history, and more. It is the relationship of each to the other that makes the leadership matrix."[5]

And there is no relationship without communication. The best-laid plans are worthless unless they're communicated to others. The best-intentioned feelings are useless to another unless they're expressed. Leaders must be able to express themselves.

But those expressions must be carefully thought out, and they must have a redemptive purpose. Many communicators have learned the hard way that some comments are better left unsaid— especially within range of the microphone. One radio announcer on a Christian radio station commented to his engineer without knowing that the microphone was still live, "I shouldn't have put that Tabasco sauce on my eggs this morning." Then, in probably his most embarrassing broadcast moment, he emitted the belch heard 'round the world!

Jesus didn't make statements that shouldn't be heard when the microphone is on. His communication was sound, purposeful, and redemptive.

Whenever Jesus spoke in public, His speech had a redeeming

value. Even when He spoke harshly to the spiritual hypocrites of His day, it came from an impassioned heart of acceptance and love. Naturally—His speech was a reflection of His character.

With His speech, He lifted people from their dungeons of despair. For example, to a guilty adulteress He gave the declaration of her independence.

The teachers of the law and the Pharisees brought in a woman caught in adultery. They made her stand before the group and said to Jesus, "Teacher, this woman was caught in the act of adultery. In the Law Moses commanded us to stone such women. Now what do you say?" They were using this question as a trap, in order to have a basis for accusing him.

But Jesus bent down and started to write on the ground with his finger. When they kept on questioning him, he straightened up and said to them, "If any one of you is without sin, let him be the first to throw a stone at her." Again he stooped down and wrote on the ground.

At this, those who heard began to go away one at a time, the older ones first, until only Jesus was left, with the woman still standing there. Jesus straightened up and asked her, "Woman, where are they? Has no one condemned you?"

"No one, sir," she said.

"Then neither do I condemn you," Jesus declared. "Go now and leave your life of sin" *(John 8:3-11)*.

With His speech Jesus gave hope to the helpless. One day as He taught, a group of His friends lowered a crippled young man from the roof into the very room where Jesus stood. He was brought there expecting to receive a miracle. Instead, he got two. In mercy, Jesus mingled healing with forgiveness in the life of the helpless. And with a word, the young man's life was forever changed. When the religious leaders questioned His actions, Jesus was patient enough to answer: "'That you may know that the Son of Man has authority on earth to forgive sins. . . .' He said to the paralyzed man, 'I tell you, get up, take your mat and go home'" (Luke 5:24).

With His speech He motivated people to use their talents for the Kingdom. "No one lights a lamp and hides it in a jar or puts it under a bed. Instead, he puts it on a stand, so that those who come in can see the light" (Luke 8:16).

But whenever He spoke, it was with sincerity and love.

Paul Davidson wrote in *USA Today* about a group of computer hackers who made a break with their dishonest past to work for a computer security firm and eventually were hired as consultants by the government. Called "L0pht," the computer specialists boasted to a Senate committee of being able to shut down the Internet in 30 minutes. Davidson wrote, "L0pht members describe themselves as 'gray hats,' on the edge between good and evil hackers."[6]

There's no room for "gray hats" in Christian leadership. If you're to call people forward in this millennium, even when they're standing still, you'll commit yourself to sincerity in your communication as well as in your conduct.

The power of a promise. You'll discover the power of a promise—the influence of keeping your word. People are motivated by Christian leaders who always try to do what they say they will. Vibrant Christian leaders understand that once a promise is given, people are waiting for the action.

Granted, that's not always possible. Circumstances sometimes seal off the promised actions like orange cones on a construction project. Sometimes the leader simply can't deliver on a promise. The promise was made too hastily; events caused a detour; facts and figures have changed. But the sincerity remains.

If you haven't already, you'll discover the fantastic power of words. Words can be used either as *bombs* or *bouquets*. Which would you rather receive at your doorstep? A few words and sentences can be forged together and lobbed into the life of another to cause as much havoc as a two-year-old at a tea party.

Conversely, you can put approximately the same amount of words and sentences together to hand a discouraged worker a "speech bouquet." In fact, "Thank you—I appreciate you," is better *said* than shown!

And words that don't lift simply ought to be left alone.

And speaking of microphones . . .

"Test, one, two. Test, one, two. Is this on?"

Most people think Christian singers and speakers can count only to two! Every meeting or concert usually begins with a sound check.

How about a sincerity check? How will you know when your communication is "sincere"? New Testament leader Paul said, "Let your conversation be always full of grace, seasoned with salt, so that you may know how to answer everyone" (Col. 4:6).

Here are some questions to use as guidelines:

- Is it honest without being petty?
- Will it bring hope or help, or will it bring hurt?
- Will the giver and the receiver be better because of it?
- Does it reflect the attitude of Jesus Christ?
- Will the receiver learn something positive from the communication?

Shady communication and see-through promises never pay dividends—only division.

The story is told of two college students who were to take a final exam. Instead of studying, they took the time to go to town for a party.

The next morning, they overslept and missed the exam. Going to their professor, they made up a very convincing and heartbreaking story of how they had gone to visit an aunt of one of the students who was ill in a nearby hospital.

"It was awful, Prof," the students explained. "After we left that poor invalid woman, we rushed home to study for our exam. It was pouring down rain, and suddenly we had a flat tire along a very busy expressway."

"Stop!" The professor interrupted. "You can make up the exam tomorrow."

The next day, the students arrived at the professor's classroom. He quickly put them in two different rooms and handed them an exam. The first part of the exam was a breeze. The note at the top of the exam paper said that Part 1 was worth 30 points.

There was also a note at the bottom: "Turn this page over for the rest of the exam—*worth 70 points.*"

Part 2 was on the other side. It was a "fill-in-the-blank" question that caused instant anxiety for the students in their separate rooms:

"Which tire went flat on your trip to see that invalid aunt?"[7]

4. Jesus was sincere in His relationships

The Gospel writers counted 5,000 men. With women and children added, the number was probably at least three times that amount. Sitting on the sunny slope of a Judean mountain, they had no idea that the sermon they were hearing would be called the greatest of history—the Sermon on the Mount. Jesus included points about meekness that turns to an inheritance, poverty that owns a kingdom, and humility that blossoms into exaltation. Timeless truths poked their heads through windows of narration, object lessons, humor, and drama.

What a magnificent day!

What a magnificent storyteller, this Nazarene!

Was it His greatest sermon? Probably. But it wasn't His only sermon. There were so many others that touched the hearts and minds of those who followed Him.

One was heard by only an audience that was tiny compared to the thousands who had heard Him on that other mountain.

This mountain scene was far removed from sunny slopes and gentle waves that caressed the trembling shores of Galilee. This sermon could barely be heard above the angry shouts of a bloodthirsty mob on Golgotha.

Near the cross of Jesus stood his mother, his mother's sister, Mary the wife of Clopas, and Mary Magdalene. When Jesus saw his mother there, and the disciple whom he loved standing nearby, he said to his mother, "Dear woman, here is your son," and to the disciple, "Here is your mother." From that time on, this disciple took her into his home *(John 19:25-27)*.

This wasn't a sermon about lights hid under bushels or hearts pure enough to see God. This was about duty. A son would soon die and leave a mother without any means of support.

Devotion won out over the commotion.

Love ruled in the face of unspeakable anger.

With one act of mercy, the greatest leader who ever lived taught His followers how to sincerely put relationships above responsibilities: "Dear woman, here is your son." And to His dear friend He gave the task of caring for the woman who bore the Messiah.

It could truly be said of Jesus that He was a "people person." He sat down to dinner with Lazarus, Martha, and Mary at Bethany. Friends and loved ones were dear to His heart.

Relationships above responsibilities. He was concerned with His earthly duties. He practiced the carpenter trade. He hung out with fishermen. He gave some of His greatest insights from the examples seen in the sheepherding and agriculture communities. But

He involved himself with those vocations to touch the lives of their people. He was concerned that fishers of *fish* become fishers of *men*.

Jay C. Grelen wrote an on-line article about basketball superstar David Robinson. After the statistics were quoted, the trophies had been counted, and the accomplishments had been acknowledged, Grelen focused on what really mattered in the life of the 7-foot-1 San Antonio Spurs standout: his family and friends. "He is more concerned that his three boys learn godly character than whether they can match his Top 10 ranking in the NBA for points, rebounds, and blocked shots per game. He is more concerned that his fans see him live out his faith than he is interested in talking about the time in 1994 that he scored 71 points against the Los Angeles Clippers."[8]

Faith. Family. Friends. Those are the lasting things.

"Let's get a move on!" an anxious husband reminded his wife as the family scurried about for the journey to Sunday school.

The tension in the room soon began to thicken like day-old bubble gum. "What?" the mother asked sharply.

The husband spoke softer and more deliberately: "I just wondered if we could try not to be late again this Sunday."

"OK," the wife replied sharply. "Let's do a trade-off."

"A trade-off?"

"Yep!" the wife continued. "Next week you cook breakfast, dress the kids, let the dog out, gather all the Sunday School quarterlies, get dinner ready . . . and I'll sit in the car, honk the horn, and shake my watch in the window!"[9]

Obviously harmony in the home should have been a priority over punctuality at the church. Now, that's not an indictment against punctuality, especially when tardiness seems to be gaining ground over baseball as the national pastime.

But Christian leaders cannot forget the Golgotha scene. Relationships are more important than responsibilities. Right in the midst of the most trying time of His life, Jesus focused on His family duties.

Whether a Christian leader builds a church or organization is ultimately not as important as whether he or she focuses on building a home. Paul asked a haunting question that rings in the ears of new millennium leaders: "If anyone does not know how to manage his own family, how can he take care of God's church?" (1 Tim. 3:5).

Never neglect your own family in your service to others.

Family life must not be an afterthought. Fifty years from this point in your life, times with your immediate family will generate greater memories than a packed auditorium on Friend Day.

A famous actor known for his devotion to his family once said, "I make a lot of money and I've given a lot of it to charities, but I've given all of myself to my wife and the kids, and that's the best donation I'll ever make."

A sincere devotion to duty—including family duties—doesn't escape the glances of people for whom you're responsible. That devotion could be the very incentive that sparks them to start a "renovation project" in their own homes. And the resulting improvements there could very well extend to your church or organization.

2 INFLUENCING WITH INTEGRITY

THE POLICE OFFICER BACKED HIS CRUISER into the alley beside the bank in a small town. He needed one more ticket to impress the new police chief.

Suddenly he spotted one of the town's senior citizens exit from the only restaurant in town, a Kentucky Fried Chicken franchise added on to the corner convenience store. Grandpa climbed into the borrowed car, his grandson's new Mustang. But he was so impressed with the car that he forgot the bucket of chicken he had placed on the rooftop.

Driving down Main Street at speeds of over 25 miles-per-hour, Grandpa drove right through the town's only stop sign.

This is my chance, the rookie officer thought as he threw the switch on the red-and-blue roof lights and started the siren wailing.

Grandpa pulled over slowly. The police officer walked briskly to the driver's side, took the bucket of chicken from the roof, and held it to the window for Grandpa to see.

Unfazed, Grandpa simply rolled down the window and said with a kindly smile, "No thanks, son—I bought a bucket for myself."

The first-century Church didn't have Kentucky Fried Chicken, but they did have a food problem. They needed a staff to serve meals in the fellowship hall. Ministry needs weren't being met; some folks missed lunch because they couldn't read the menu. If you were one of the disciples making the recruitment choice, what would you look for in a worker?

Good communication skills?

Ability to do basic math?

Pleasant smile?

Good language skills?

Neat appearance?

Stellar work ethic?

Able to get along with others?

Probably. These are all good "waiter" traits. But here's how they settled on their choice:

> In those days when the number of disciples was increasing, the Grecian Jews among them complained against the Hebraic Jews because their widows were being overlooked in the daily distribution of food. So the Twelve gathered all the disciples together and said, "It would not be right for us to neglect the ministry of the word of God in order to wait on tables. Brothers, choose seven men from among you who are known to be full of the Spirit and wisdom. We will turn this responsibility over to them and will give our attention to prayer and the ministry of the word."
>
> This proposal pleased the whole group. They chose Stephen, a man full of faith and of the Holy Spirit; also Philip, Procorus, Nicanor, Timon, Parmenas, and Nicolas from Antioch, a convert to Judaism. They presented these men to the apostles, who prayed and laid their hands on them (*Acts 6:1-6*).

If you're going to do the work of the Kingdom, if you're going to help it move forward on earth, there's something more important than how you look, how you talk, what you wear, what you can do, and where you've been.

Who you are is more important than all the rest! Personal integrity is the main issue.

INTEGRITY IS A LEGACY

A television sitcom promo included an interesting statement by the main character: "I learned about integrity from my father. He had five wives but never missed an alimony payment."

If worldly integrity is learned by the example of careless character, then the Church is called to live a step above. A Christian worker's integrity speaks louder than a "sharp" résumé, a handful of brochures, or a stack of business cards. Integrity is one thing that can't be handed to you as you walk across a graduation platform. You don't hang it on a wall—you treasure it in your heart.

Integrity comes from within. It's the result of focused faith, godly choices, right associations, and a tenacious commitment to truth.

When it's there, in the life of God's servant, it's beautiful. When it's missing, it's messy! It very well may be one of the least-recognized gifts for new millennium ministry. All we have to do is look around the landscape of our times to see that many have tried to lead without it—and sadly, some have had a degree of success.

But later on, when the historians think about those leaders, they'll struggle to remember how many people they had on their staff. They will have forgotten how many letters followed their names. They'll try to recall how many perspiring children they once packed onto a Sunday School bus. Probably they will have forgotten how many small groups they wrung out of their big churches, and they'll have to search for the figures on their financial reports. But they'll remember whether or not they were persons of integrity.

Integrity follows you like that high school picture you've been trying to keep out of circulation at your class reunions.

In a publication called *The Cross and the Flag,* the legacy of integrity was chronicled:

Max Jukes lived in New York State: he was an unbeliever. Jukes married a girl of like character and training. From this union came 1,029 descendants.

- Three hundred died prematurely. Of the ones that lived, 100 were sent to the penitentiary for an average of 13 years each.
- One hundred and ninety were public prostitutes.
- One hundred were alcoholics.
- The family cost the state $1,200,000 and made no contribution to society.

Jonathan Edwards lived in the same state. He believed in God and Christian training. He married a girl of like character. From this union, 729 descendants were traced.

- Three hundred became preachers.
- Sixty-five became college professors.
- Thirteen were presidents of universities.
- Sixty became authors.
- Three were elected to Congress, and one became vice president of the United States.

When it comes to Kingdom work, integrity can't be faked. Like the incident in the first-century Church, sooner or later a waiter will need to be chosen to work in the fellowship hall. Eventually someone will need the stuff it takes to do the least significant work in a church or organization with excellence, and suddenly it will become obvious: What's needed is someone full of faith and of the Holy Spirit.

Esteemed business consultant Fred Smith wrote,

> One principle I've learned is that God will not do for me what I can do for myself, but he will not let me do for myself what only he can do. God has given me intelligence and created my opportunities—I have a responsibility to use my gifts fully. If I'm not willing to do that, God has no obligation to add his blessing to what I do. On the other hand, when I try to accomplish by human means what can be done only by spiritual means, I embezzle God's authority.[1]

INTEGRITY HOLDS US

Since he was chosen first, Stephen must have been a person of noted integrity. "They chose Stephen, a man full of faith and of the Holy Spirit." Of Hellenistic origin, his name means "crown." Biblical history says that he was a staunch defender of the faith who stood against the religious leaders of his day. His message: ceremony and law were fulfilled in the person of the Messiah, the Lord Jesus Christ. Of course, his religious "defiance" resulted in his arrest and later his martyrdom.

At his trial the heavens opened for a sneak preview, as if to honor his spiritual integrity and to prepare him for his welcome: "Stephen, full of the Holy Spirit, looked up to heaven and saw the glory of God, and Jesus standing at the right hand of God. 'Look,' he said, 'I see heaven open and the Son of Man standing at the right hand of God'" (Acts 7:55-56).

Notice that he was still "full of the Holy Spirit." After all the rigors and riots of his tumultuous ministry, his faith was as strong at the last as it was at the beginning. Integrity is not just something we hold on to—it's something that holds us.

INTEGRITY IS CONTAGIOUS

And what is integrity's influence? The Scriptures remind us in the same incident:

At this they covered their ears and, yelling at the top of their voices, they all rushed at him, dragged him out of the city and began to stone him. Meanwhile, the witnesses laid their clothes at the feet of a young man named Saul.

While they were stoning him, Stephen prayed, "Lord Jesus, receive my spirit." Then he fell on his knees and cried out, "Lord, do not hold this sin against them." When he had said this, he fell asleep *(Acts 7:57-60)*.

We can't help but notice one of the witnesses of that awful execution. "[They] laid their clothes at the feet of a young man named Saul." Named Paul after his conversion, the New Testament giant in the faith learned about devotion on that day. Watching the execution of the first Christian martyr, he took a minicourse at the College of Commitment.

Would he ever be able to forget that awesome scene? Would he be able to overlook the shine on Stephen's face, or would those words "Lord, do not hold this sin against them" ever stop ringing in his ears? Obviously not. Paul would later exhibit the very same integrity in his own life.

Integrity lingers. As Paul dog-paddled in the icy waters of the sea following his shipwreck, perhaps he was warmed by the remembrance of that glow of glory on Stephen's face. As he faced the cruelty and loneliness of the Roman dungeons, perhaps Stephen's song of forgiveness played in his heart like a sweet symphony.

You see, once you encounter integrity at its Spirit-anointed best, you can never really forget it.

INTEGRITY: THE MARK OF NEW TESTAMENT LEADERSHIP

Integrity was characteristic of those who followed the Master. Early Church ministries were marked with the impressions made by good and godly people—people who hated evil and clung to the good. It was almost as if it were in the job description for New Testament leadership. When Philip the disciple enlisted his brother to be a follower of Jesus, the Master saw something in the new recruit that should be characteristic of new millennium followers. "When Jesus saw Nathanael approaching, he said of him, 'Here is a true Israelite, in whom there is nothing false'" (John 1:47).

You can't hide integrity. Nathanael was known for telling the truth. If that's the only thing that can be said about your leadership, it's enough!

Fred Smith also wrote of listening to the sermon tapes of a well-known speaker who had left the ministry. When asked what he thought of him, Smith replied, "I greatly admired his technical ability, his research, his eloquence and delivery, but I never sensed in his sermons spiritual power. I felt he was spiritually impotent. I kept wanting to feel the presence of the Spirit, which I never did." Smith added, "He later divorced his wife and left the ministry, not from lack of talent, with which he was greatly blessed, but from lack of spiritual power."[2]

Contrast that with the news report of the apostles' New Testament ministry: "With great power the apostles continued to testify to the resurrection of the Lord Jesus, and much grace was upon them all" (Acts 4:33).

There are at least three areas of a leader's life in which integrity must be exhibited—in which a leader must hate what is evil and cling to the good. Of course, they're not exclusive areas, because character is interwoven into our life like threads in a beautiful tapestry, and when it's displayed, the individual strands are lost in the overall beauty. But these three areas call for qualities that every Christian leader must possess if he or she would influence people and lead them forward: personal integrity, spiritual integrity, and institutional integrity.

PERSONAL INTEGRITY

Can you imagine seeking a guide to lead you on a dangerous mountain climbing expedition and reading the following classified ad?

Carpet-layer seeks new employment as mountain climbing guide. Not afraid of heights; willing to learn on the job. Fee negotiable. References provided following first climb.

Hiring a guide with those qualifications would make just as much sense as a church or organization putting their confidence in a leader that has never risen to a level of personal excellence. Christian leaders will never lead people to a height they have never climbed personally.

Another classified ad for a lifeguard turned up only one applicant. A six-foot-eight-inch-tall young man stepped to the counter and announced, "I'm here about the lifeguard job."

The recruiter asked, "Can you swim?"

The applicant replied, "No, but I can wade pretty far out!"

Mr. Webster says that "integrity" includes three aspects: incorruptibility, soundness, and completeness.[3]

Personal integrity begins with good personal habits

Integrity clings to the good. John Maxwell said, "Anyone can say that he has integrity, but action is the real indicator of character. Your character determines who you are. Who you are determines what you see. What you see determines what you do. That's why you can never separate a leader's character from his actions."[4]

"Don't forget to brush your teeth," Mom reminds after her goodnight hug. Why? It isn't just a dentistry issue. Sure, she knows that the prevention of tooth decay is important, but she also knows that regular brushing is a discipline that will blend into the other areas of the child's life as well.

Personal integrity is born in the practices of personal discipline: tooth-brushing today, truth-telling tomorrow!

"Any luck?" the friendly bystander asked a fisherman slouching over the side of a rickety dock.

"Not today," the fisherman replied sadly. Then he stood up and added excitedly, "But yesterday was outstanding! I caught 14 bluegill, 10 trout, and 26 perch! I went so far over the limit that I just quit counting."

"Is that right?" the bystander responded.

"Sure is!" the fisherman said.

The man replied, "That's interesting. Let me introduce myself. I'm the game warden." Then he reached out his hand and added, "And who might you be?"

The fisherman quickly responded, "John Doe's the name. I'm the president of the local Liars' Club!"

No Christian leader ought to be a member of the Liars' Club. But he or she ought to be president of the Truth Club. The practice of excellence in the consistent telling of the truth is a primary example of personal integrity.

That was exemplified in a recent newspaper account. A noted

historian and Pulitzer prize-winning author admitted that his years of teaching and writing about his military service had been a sham. His stories about military exploits in Vietnam were all fabricated. Placed on leave by the renowned college where he had taught for nearly 30 years, the professor made a public apology for misleading the students and faculty.

Maxie Dunnam wrote in *Leading with Vision,* "Your public identity comes from the nature of your calling, your biblical understandings, and your personal faith roots. But your personal identity must be rooted in who you really are. All the permanent fruits and lasting progress that result from your leadership are based on strong character."[5]

Paul taught the importance of developing character by personal discipline in his letter to New Testament Church leader Timothy: "God did not give us a spirit of timidity, but a spirit of power, of love and of self-discipline" (2 Tim. 1:7). In other words, God's *grace* and our *grit* are a winning combination! And it applies in all areas of life in which we must cling to the good.

Integrity clings to good grooming habits. Would you expect to see the ambassador of a foreign country represent that country at a public gathering dressed in the clothes that he or she wore to work in the garden? Of course not! The ambassador's *apparel* is a reflection of the ambassador's *association.*

Persons who seek to move people forward are reminded: "We are therefore Christ's ambassadors, as though God were making his appeal through us" (2 Cor. 5:20).

Certainly it must be noted that this is the age of "casual Fridays" in the workplace and "informal Sundays" in the worship center. But Christian leaders will still exercise caution when it comes to their appearance. They will be

- freshly showered
- properly minted
- appropriately clothed
- decisively shod
- neatly coiffed

The shabbiest-looking person in a hospital room shouldn't be the visitor from the local church! The visitor is there as an ambassador of the kingdom of God. And ambassadors aren't usually seen at public gatherings wearing flip-flops and tank tops.

Integrity clings to good diet, exercise, and rest habits. For some, an intense exercise program might include sitting in a bathtub, filling it with water, pulling the plug, and then fighting the current! Thankfully, others have more variety in their exercise program. Author Max Lucado reminds, "God has a high regard for your body. You should as well. Respect it. I did not say worship it. But I did say respect it. It is, after all, the temple of God. Be careful how you feed it, use it, and maintain it. You wouldn't want anyone trashing your home; God doesn't want anyone trashing his."[6]

For the Christian, dietary temperance is obviously a good thing. And the balance is probably somewhere between kosher and Krispy Kremes! Once again, the apostle Paul gives us some guidelines: "I beat my body and make it my slave so that after I have preached to others, I myself will not be disqualified for the prize" (1 Cor. 9:27).

And don't forget that nap! Cutting-edge leadership may hinge on an extra hour or two of rest. Some need very little rest, and others need far more than they think! In his on-line *Tuesday* column, educator and columnist Keith Drury warned of the danger zones facing people in high-profile ministries:

> All of us in ministry are overworked; it is an occupational hazard. But the big guys are really overworked! They burn the candle at both ends. . . . They are high energy, do the work of two (or five) others, stay up late, get up early, travel all over the place, and generally get more exhausted than the rest of us. . . . Sleep deprivation has two effects: (1) a similar effect as alcohol on impairing judgment. Big guys who aren't sleeping enough are more likely to do dumb things than a minister who has a regular eight hours of Zs in the bank. But that's not all. (2) Sleep deprivation erodes one's strength of will. . . . They sometimes seek from God a "work of grace" to accomplish what sleep was supposed to do.[7]

Integrity clings to good study habits. Elmer Towns wrote of the qualities of a leader, "The great leader has mental ability to seize and use information from a wide variety of sources. As I interview great church leaders, I have noticed how many have an incredible amount of knowledge. They know, they see, they remember, they connect concepts, and they use information they have gathered both formally and informally from many people and places."[8]

- Read for personal enrichment, not just for research.
- Read widely, not just from one author's work.
- Read systematically—schedule regular reading times.
- Read faithfully—filter reading through biblical principles.
- Read with discretion—watch out for secular philosophy.

The Internet has opened a vast storehouse of information that a Christian leader may utilize. Visit a web site, type in a search word, click the mouse, and in a matter of minutes you can be traversing the ethereal aisles of the world's great libraries.

But with another click, you can be sneaking through the dark alleys of cyberporn peddlers and prostitutes. The casualty count is rising at an alarming rate. It's open season for undisciplined travelers in cyberspace. Hell's agenda is to take the good and turn it into the bad and the ugly. E-researchers must build a safety system into their surfing:

- Install a reliable Internet filter.
- Place the computer in a prominent location.
- Start your Internet session with prayer.
- Let a ministry buddy review your cybertrail on a regular basis.
- Delete adult-oriented ads quickly (don't even "investigate" them).
- Use Christian "web portals" as your Internet entrance.
- Stay away from chat rooms.
- Avoid surfing when you're tired or stressed out.
- Avoid working in a remote environment.

Integrity clings to good financial habits. There are times when a Christian leader's integrity is compromised in the checkout lane of the corner store. A charge card under the control of the "natural man" is as dangerous as a gorilla with a grudge and an acute case of indigestion!

The apostle Peter wrote to New Testament leaders, "Be shepherds of God's flock that is under your care, serving as overseers—not because you must, but because you are willing, as God wants you to be; not greedy for money, but eager to serve" (1 Pet. 5:2). In other words, don't let your ministry be controlled by your money!

- Guard your credit rating.
- Develop a savings plan.
- Learn to resist the "irresistibles."
- Plan today to retire tomorrow.

Cling to good thoughts. The apostle's well-worn advice is still cutting-edge instruction: "Whatever is true, whatever is noble, whatever is right, whatever is pure, whatever is lovely, whatever is admirable—if anything is excellent or praiseworthy—think about such things" (Phil. 4:8).

Some Christians are about as positive as an auto muffler salesman! Gloom clouds follow them like the dust cloud trailing Charlie Brown's buddy Pigpen. Everyone who walks into a room has an opportunity to either darken or brighten it. Vibrant Christian leaders have disciplined themselves to be "room brighteners"—you might say they have a fluorescent faith. Their positive attitude inspires people rather than incites them.

SPIRITUAL INTEGRITY

One of the great mentor-mentored relationships in the New Testament was that of Paul and his spiritual son, Timothy. Bundled together, his letters to the young pastor are a ministry manual.

On one occasion, the mentor gave a wonderful word of advice that may be applied to this matter of spiritual integrity: "Don't let anyone look down on you because you are young, but set an example for the believers in speech, in life, in love, in faith and in purity" (1 Tim. 4:12).

The issue of his youthfulness was only part of the reminder. The meatier portion of the advice is in Paul's focus on Timothy's life resulting from his faith. He urged him to be a living example of "faith" and "purity"—a traveling exhibit of what God can do with a surrendered life.

Spiritual integrity doesn't come with a subscription to someone's tape ministry. It comes from a heart that makes an effort to love God with all its might. In Matt. 22:37 Jesus quoted the great commandment: "Love the Lord your God with all your heart and with all your soul and with all your mind."

Tim Bowman wrote:

> The first time Jesus addresses greatness in His kingdom surfaces in Matt. 5:19. He says that "anyone who breaks one of the least of these commandments and teaches others to do the same

will be called least in the kingdom of heaven, but whoever practices and teaches these commands will be called great in the kingdom of heaven."

The first measure of greatness, then, is obedience. . . . Jesus commands us to anchor our ministries in personal obedience. It is a measure of significance that is as accessible and demanding to the pastor of 50 as the pastor of 5,000. I have discovered that the pastorate, with its temptation toward a righteous facade, nibbles away at my attention to personal obedience.[9]

Putting first things first

> Give God the first minutes of every day in prayer,
> Give God the first day of the week,
> Give God the first consideration in every decision,
> Give God the first portion of every paycheck,
> Give God the first place in your heart.
>
> —North Carolina West *Wesleyan*

New Testament leaders practiced the principles of the Word of God when it came to their spiritual lives. Of course, that's why they were people of spiritual integrity. Here is some of the advice they followed:

1. Talk to the Lord. The New Testament church at Thessalonica was called to prayer. Their prayer advice forms a pattern for every New Testament leader: "Night and day we pray most earnestly that we may see you again and supply what is lacking in your faith" (1 Thess. 3:10).

The Church was born in a prayer meeting (Acts 4:31), and prayer meetings have been its source of power throughout her history. The "gospel ship" simply has to be in touch with the Harbormaster if it's going to successfully navigate the rough seas of this millennium.

There is currently a heart hunger that has not been satisfied by unlimited charge cards or unrestrained behavior. The bright lights of the world have illuminated the broken spirits of a people who have traded a real song for a mere tune.

And God has planted His workers in the midst of it all! He has called us to harvest souls amid the weeds and the ruins.

But first He calls us to prayer. As Jesus said in Mark 14:38, "Watch and pray so that you will not fall into temptation. The spirit is willing, but the body is weak." He invites us to strengthen our personal integrity by the eternal flow of His supply.

Little "Now I lay me down to sleep" prayers won't be enough. If Christians are going to carry the credentials of the Christ with any credibility in this crisis-filled age, they will have to be in constant touch with Him. And they will stand the tallest when they're on their knees.

2. Spend time in the Word. New Testament leader Peter told the Church to "always be prepared to give an answer to everyone who asks you to give the reason for the hope that you have" (1 Pet. 3:15).

Spiritual integrity, then, owes its authenticity to faithful knowledge. Give us a fresh touch of "Jesus loves me! this I know, / For the Bible tells me so."

Read the Word—

- *Prayerfully.* "The law of the LORD is perfect, reviving the soul" (Ps. 19:7*a*).
- *Thoughtfully.* "The statutes of the LORD are trustworthy, making wise the simple" (v. 7*b*).
- *Joyfully.* "The precepts of the LORD are right, giving joy to the heart" (v. 8*a*).
- *Honestly.* "The commands of the LORD are radiant, giving light to the eyes" (v. 8*b*).
- *Confidently.* "The ordinances of the LORD are sure and altogether righteous" (v. 9*b*).

3. Develop a giving channel. The Christians at Corinth were advised, "Each man should give what he has decided in his heart to give, not reluctantly or under compulsion, for God loves a cheerful giver" (2 Cor. 9:7). That's good advice for Christians in any city or time.

Giving is a source of spiritual life. All you have to do is take a whiff of a stagnant pool that has no runoff, and you will quickly envision the benefits of giving.

Paul reminded New Testament leaders not to jeopardize their integrity by falling behind in their own generosity. "Just as you excel in everything—in faith, in speech, in knowledge, in complete earnestness and in your love for us—see that you also excel in this grace of giving" (2 Cor. 8:7).

4. Win souls. Timothy was given an interesting job description by his supervisor: "Keep your head in all situations, endure hardship, do the work of an evangelist, discharge all the duties of your ministry" (2 Tim. 4:5). In other words,

- Stay cool, even in the furnace: "Keep your head in all situations."
- Don't ask for a way out—ask for a way through: "Endure hardship."
- Win souls: "Do the work of an evangelist."
- Don't quit until you're finished: "Discharge all the duties of your ministry."

Sadly, in many religious organizations the Four Spiritual Laws have been replaced with the Three Excuses: "Busy, busy, busy!" Paperwork, properties, and personnel problems hang around the neck of the new millennium leader like a pendent made out of a stuffed pachyderm!

Humongous responsibilities leave many leaders buried like a bone in the backyard. But even in the midst of our busywork, the fact remains that the Great Commission hasn't been amended (or even sent to a congressional committee). "Go into all the world and preach the good news to all creation. Whoever believes and is baptized will be saved, but whoever does not believe will be condemned" (Mark 16:15-16).

Granted, the work of an administrator is important. Where there is no *administrator,* papers won't get properly shuffled. And where there is no *administrator,* parking lots won't get paved. But where there is no *evangelist,* people won't get saved!

Rom. 10:14 says, "How, then, can they call on the one they have not believed in? And how can they believe in the one of whom they have not heard? And how can they hear without someone preaching to them?"

Spiritual integrity has at its very core the conviction that people without a personal saving relationship with the Lord Jesus Christ are lost! And it must somehow rise to the surface of responsibilities in the life of a Christian leader.

James Earl Massey wrote, "The Church began under a leader with the highest integrity: Jesus of Nazareth, a teaching preacher. Intent on developing an effective working group for ministry in the world, Christ fashioned a community that looked to God, trusted His judgment, and had eyes of vision for claiming the world."[10]

5. Learn to say yes and no. Someone once said sarcastically, "Don't worry about biting off more than you can chew—your mouth is probably a whole lot bigger than you think." But the problem of biting off more than we can chew *administratively* is nothing to snicker about!

Jesus said, "Simply let your 'Yes' be 'Yes,' and your 'No,' 'No'; anything beyond this comes from the evil one" (Matt. 5:37). Of course, the immediate message from the Master is to avoid wholesale promises that are impossible to keep. But the second-tier message is this: Be careful about commitments.

Too few, or too many, commitments can stain the résumé of a Christian leader like spilled coffee. Learning to say yes or no based upon a careful evaluation of time, resources, and other responsibilities is a mark of personal character. "Yes" is a word that flows like well water from the lips of most workers. But "No" sort of hangs in our mouth like porcupine pudding.

And sometimes our overworked "Yes" comes from a loyal and sincere heart. In a writing from the Josephson Institute of Ethics reprinted in the magazine of the National Religious Broadcasters, the author reminded,

> Loyalty is a tricky thing. It is not uncommon for friends, employers, coworkers and others who have a claim on us to demand that their interests be ranked first, even above ethical considerations. Loyalty is a reciprocal concept, however, and no one has the right to ask another to sacrifice ethical principles in the name of a special relationship. Indeed, one forfeits a claim of loyalty when so high a price is put on maintaining the relationship.[11]

6. Guard your purity. New Testament leaders are called to live extreme lives—above the reproach of the world.

> Teach the older men to be temperate, worthy of respect, self-controlled, and sound in faith, in love and in endurance. Likewise, teach the older women to be reverent in the way they live, not to be slanderers or addicted to much wine, but to teach what is good. Then they can train the younger women to love their husbands and children, to be self-controlled and pure, to be busy at home, to be kind, and to be subject to their husbands, so that no one will malign the word of God. Similarly, encourage the young men to be self-controlled (*Titus 2:2-6*).

So personal integrity in the life of the Christian leader is not only about religious beliefs and responsibilities but also about relationships. It's here in the arena of interpersonal relationships that integrity is often put to its greatest test. The very nature of our proximity to other Christians puts us in a very precarious situation.

- Our counseling sessions expose inner feelings to someone other than a spouse.
- Our ministries often place us in team situations that are mutually exclusive.
- Our expressions of Christian love and concern can be misinterpreted by those who are emotionally needy.
- Our heartfelt compassion may possibly turn to human passion.
- Our world environment encourages selfish behavior.

There are some proven steps that a Christian leader can take to reduce personal risk:

1. *Watch what you watch.* Don't let the influences of a godless society park themselves in your TV screen, your computer monitor, or your mind.
2. *Stay close to Jesus.* Cultivate a daily walk with the Lord.
3. *Find an accountability partner.* Choose someone of the same sex whom you can confide in—one who will not only keep your confidence but also be faithful in praying for you.
4. *Address relational problems with your spouse* rather than a third party—especially a member of the opposite sex. Work on solving family problems before they become even more divisive.
5. *Keep a check on your stress level.* Don't let overwork make you vulnerable.
6. *Whenever possible, minister with your spouse.*

A lifetime of service can be jeopardized by a moment of selfishness. But the good news is that God is faithful! As we draw near to Him, His resources are revealed to us in even greater measure.

There are some additional and positive steps to maintaining interpersonal integrity:

Be gracious—Give honor to whom honor is due.

Be positive—Make people feel good about being around you.

Be courteous—Don't forget the "magic words."

Be truthful—Never hedge the facts.

Be kind—Do unto others.

Be aware—Look for ways you can be of service.

Be thankful—Don't make people search for your appreciation.

7. Stay focused on your vision. Vision and purpose are marks of personal integrity. A leader with a Spirit-led direction cannot afford to be sidetracked by "incidentalism."

Leighton Ford wrote, "Desires to serve God, to help others to find personal fulfillment are all so intertwined that it is difficult to separate them. . . . From time to time, we need to pull aside from our busy activities and involvements and think about what we are doing and why we are doing it."[12]

INSTITUTIONAL INTEGRITY

Leadership is often lonely. But it's not lonely just at the top of the ladder; it's often lonely at every other rung. Paul must have felt as if he had failed a Dale Carnegie course at one point:

> Do your best to come to me quickly, for Demas, because he loved this world, has deserted me and has gone to Thessalonica. Crescens has gone to Galatia, and Titus to Dalmatia. Only Luke is with me. . . . I sent Tychicus to Ephesus. . . . Alexander the metalworker did me a great deal of harm. The Lord will repay him for what he has done. You too should be on your guard against him, because he strongly opposed our message. At my first defense, no one came to my support, but everyone deserted me. May it not be held against them (*2 Tim. 4:9-12, 14-16*).

Former president George Bush gave some good advice to leaders:

> *First,* no matter how hard-fought the issue, never get personal . . .

> *Second,* do your homework. You can't lead without knowing what you are talking about. . . .

> *Third,* the American legislative process is one of give and take. Use your power as a leader to persuade, not intimidate. . . .

> *Fourth,* be considerate of the needs of your colleagues, even if they're at the bottom of the totem pole.[13]

Leaders need all the advice they can get—and sometimes get more than they want!

As captain of the organizational vessel, you are responsible to
chart the course
recruit the sailors
keep the sails up
watch out for the rocks
and get ready to put everyone else into the lifeboats first!

The integrity of your "vessel" is most often a reflection of your
own personal integrity. So great caution should be taken to make
sure your organization "stands tall" in the Kingdom or in the community.

1. Stay on track. More than likely you have taken time to construct a statement of purpose—documenting the "whats," the
"whys," and the "wherefores" of your organization. Your next important task will be to keep your organization on that "purpose track."
Paul encouraged New Testament leaders to stay on the same page.
"Make my joy complete by being like-minded, having the same
love, being one in spirit and purpose" (Phil. 2:2). Make sure the activities, schedules, and services complement the very reason your
organization is around in the first place.

2. Don't advertise something you can't deliver. The integrity
of many churches or organizations has been tarnished by 100-dollar
ads for 10-dollar programs! If it's not going to be the "best," "big-
gest," "most spectacular," "heavenly" event on the face of the earth,
then don't promise it.

3. Treat staff with respect. As someone once said, "You're not
only known by the company you keep—you're also known by how
you keep your company." Your encouragement, compassion, training, support, and prayer for your workers will soon be well known
in your community. They'll also hear about "staff abuse" in a hurry!

4. Be open about plans and programs. Some leaders act as
though they're conducting an undercover operation. A lack of pub-
licity about organizational programs or plans is a surefire integrity
killer. One of the authors was invited by a pastor to be a staff member of a church—but the pastor neglected to tell the board or the
members! You can imagine the embarrassment of that prospective
staff member when he arrived on the scene. Not only was the staff
position not offered, but the senior pastor lost his parking place
within a couple of months!

5. Keep the financial books open. People want to be informed when the cash "flows" and when the cash "ebbs." One of the most important documents that an organization can publish is its financial report.

6. Protect the purity of the workers. The Christian leader must be sensitive to creating a wholesome ministry environment. Schedule ministry in group settings rather than in two-by-two settings. Encourage—and even demand—that ministry workers take regular time off. Guard the conversational times to avoid "borderline" joking and conversations.

7. Focus on the main thing. Christian organizations have as their mandated purpose the winning of souls and the building-up of believers. Bake-sale and ceramics-class sidetracks are viable only as long as they eventually lead everyone back to the main track.

War hero and former president of the United States Dwight D. Eisenhower said, "If a man's associates find him guilty of phoniness, if they find that he lacks forthright integrity, he will fail. His teachings and actions must square with each other. The first great need, therefore, is integrity and high purpose."[14]

3 FOCUSING ON THE FAMILY

THERE SHE STOOD in the line at the post office—a line that wound its way almost to the front door. A fellow customer spoke to the elderly lady waiting to buy some stamps. "Ma'am, you must be very tired—did you know there's a stamp machine over there in the corner?" he said, pointing to the machine built into the wall.

"Why, yes—thank you," the lady replied, "but I'll just wait here a little while longer. I'm getting close to the window."

The customer insisted: "But it would be so much easier for you to avoid this long line and buy your stamps at the machine."

The lady patted him on the arm and answered, "Oh, I know, but that ol' machine would never ask me how my squash was doing."

Christian leaders would be well advised to spend less time on organizational machinery and more time asking gardeners about the condition of their squash. Paul told New Testament leaders to "be devoted to one another."

People first!

Of course, programs aren't self-sustaining any more than Chevys are self-driving. There has to be someone steering, or soon there will be a crash. But programs are "personed" by flesh and blood—very human people who weep and laugh, and scorn and smile; people who hide their hurts like Easter eggs and wait eagerly for someone to look for them. Plans and programs without people are simply paper dreams. It's the *pulse* and *perspiration* that puts them into motion, not just *ideas* and *inspiration*.

People first!

Timothy was obviously a "people first" leader. His supervisor, Paul, verified it in a letter to the Christians at Philippi:

> I hope in the Lord Jesus to send Timothy to you soon, that I also may be cheered when I receive news about you. I have no one else like him, who takes a genuine interest in your welfare. For everyone looks out for his own interests, not those of Jesus

Christ. But you know that Timothy has proved himself, because as a son with his father he has served with me in the work of the gospel (*Phil. 2:19-22*).

"There's no one else like him," Paul bragged.

No one with such charisma?

No one with such a grasp of the Scriptures?

No one with such leadership potential?

No. "I have no one else like him, who takes a genuine interest in [people]"—no one who is so concerned with people that they would put the interests of others above their own advancement.

MANAGEMENT IS PERSONAL

The best managers don't sit on high horses. They help clean the stalls.

Youth with a Mission staffer Denny Gunderson wrote, "The proper—and most effective—setting for teaching others about Christian leadership is found in simple, everyday activities by which the practical and relevant nature of a relationship with God can be modeled. The servant leader must think, eat, breathe, and sleep *modeling,* for it is the medium for training future leaders."[1]

Those are the same leadership links seen in Paul's comments about Timothy: (1) "Everyone looks out for his own interests, not those of Jesus Christ," (2) "Timothy has proved himself, because as a son with his father he has served with me in the work of the gospel."

Before Timothy "did" leadership, he first "saw" leadership. And the leadership he *saw* was linked to the faith the apostle Paul *modeled*—one that Timothy personally adopted. His love for others came from his sincere love for Christ, seen first in the life of the apostle. Again, Gunderson writes, "In the New Testament context, leadership implies discipleship, and discipleship as modeled by Jesus applies to *all* areas of a person's life. It is impossible, therefore, for a leader to disciple someone else when he is seen only in a 'hero' role."[2]

MANAGEMENT IS SERVICE-ORIENTED

The leadership that moves mountains is willing to tie the shoe-laces of an excavator. And speaking of shoes, John the Baptist said, "I baptize you with water for repentance. But after me will come one who is more powerful than I, whose sandals I am not fit to carry. He will baptize you with the Holy Spirit and with fire" (Matt. 3:11). From the personal testimony and modeling of the New Testament prophet, we have all learned that one act of humble service is more powerful than a hundred PowerPoint presentations.

Entrepreneur Mary Kay Ash said, "Everyone has an invisible sign hanging from his neck saying 'Make Me Feel Important!' Never forget this message when working with people."[3]

People first!

When two of Jesus' disciples, James and John, played the classic "Who's on first?" game, the rest of the disciples probably wanted to send them to the dugout. Instead of a harsh lecture, however, Jesus gave them all a lesson in humble leadership.

> Jesus called them together and said, "You know that those who are regarded as rulers of the Gentiles lord it over them, and their high officials exercise authority over them. Not so with you. Instead, whoever wants to become great among you must be your servant, and whoever wants to be first must be slave of all. For even the Son of Man did not come to be served, but to serve, and to give his life as a ransom for many" *(Mark 10:42-45)*.

MODELING THE "PEOPLE FIRST" PRINCIPLE

The story is told of a rather irreverent man who called the church office to make a donation from the estate of his deceased uncle. When the part-time secretary answered, the man said gruffly, "Hey, this is Joe Schmedlap. Is the head hog of this-here pigpen in his office?"

Rather flabbergasted, the secretary responded, "Excuse me?"

"You know," the man continued, "is the preacher of this-here church around?"

"Oh, you mean Pastor Rivers," the secretary replied, trying to add a little dignity to the moment—and attempting to shelter her boss, who was studying.

"Whatever!" the caller said. "I've got court orders to give your church $50,000 on behalf of my uncle who just croaked."

The secretary quickly turned the conversation—"Well, in that case, please hold while I get ol' Porky on the line!"

A little more protocol, and that church would have missed a sizable contribution to the new-keyboards-for-the-praise-team fund. In fact, $50,000 would go a long way toward seating a rented orchestra on the platform for the remainder of the church year!

Putting people above plans and programs (or protocol) is another important principle for developing New Testament leaders.

The models are everywhere—even at the corner kennel.

1. The puppy principle

If you want to know how to put *people first,* study the actions and reactions of a puppy. Now, before you ask for a refund on the purchase of this book, let us explain. Puppies have the characteristics that "people first" leaders simply need to possess.

A. Puppies are more concerned with your presence than they are with your past. When the caregiver walks through the door, there's a welcome in the puppy's demeanor that makes the trip worthwhile.

Puppies are forgiving by nature. Puppies don't ask you where you've been. They don't care what time you were supposed to be home. And they don't care what you've done or how you did it. They don't even ask if you experienced any road rage along the way home. They're just glad to see you.

Paul told New Testament Christians at Ephesus, "Be kind and compassionate to one another, forgiving each other, just as in Christ God forgave you" (Eph. 4:32). In other words, "cut people some slack." Puppies love you for who you are. And they're quick to overlook what you've done.

This isn't a call to "cheap grace." It's a reminder of *great* grace! We forgive the foibles and failures of those for whom we are responsible simply because we've been on the receiving end of the Cross.

The story is told of a young boy walking along the sidewalk of a busy city. He was carrying a small birdcage with a tiny sparrow inside. When he got to the intersection, he waited for the "Walk" signal. A tall man stood alongside him waiting for the same signal and asked, "Where are you going with that bird?"

The boy replied, "I caught it. It was trapped inside a window screen at my friend's house. I'm taking it home for my cat."

"Won't your cat be cruel to that sparrow?" the man asked.

The boy replied mischievously, "Oh, that'll be fun. My cat will have a time with that bird!"

The stranger asked, "How much do you want for it?"

"I'm not planning to sell it," the boy replied. "I want to see what that cat will do to it."

The stranger reached into his pocket and pulled out a $20 bill. "This is all I have on me, but I'd like to buy that sparrow."

"Why?" the boy questioned.

"You'll see," the stranger answered. "Is it a deal?"

"Well, I could use the 20," the boy responded as he handed the birdcage to the stranger. "It's a deal."

The man traded the 20 dollars for the sparrow in the cage.

"Whatcha gonna do with it?" the boy persisted.

"Watch," the man answered. He then held the birdcage high over his head and spoke softly to the frightened sparrow, "I bought you with all I had. And now you're free."

The tender stranger opened the door of the cage, and the sparrow flew away.

That's the Cross. Satan had us caged in contempt and destined for a horrible death. At the intersection of time, a loving God asked, "How much do you want for that soul?"

The Enemy replied, "I'm not planning to sell it. It was trapped, and I found it. But what will You give me?"

And the Lord of the universe reached into the deep pockets of heaven and pulled out all He had—His own Son. Satan responded, "It's a deal! Oh, by the way, what are You going to do with that soul?"

"You'll see," the Father replied. The terrible transaction was made on a Golgotha hill. And God whispered softly to sinful souls like ours, "I bought you with all I had. Now you may go free."

B. Puppies are terrible at hiding their agendas. Puppies simply give for the sake of giving. Their awkward efforts of sloppy kisses, jumped-up greetings, and wagged tails are genuine.

"Dear Fred," the pouting letter-writer penned to her boyfriend, "I've been so upset since I broke up with you that I haven't been able to eat or watch TV. The more I think about our relationship, the more I realize how important you are to me."

And just to add a touch of tenderness, she let a drop from her water bottle drip onto the pink page of her embossed letterhead, hoping Fred would think it was a tearstain. She continued: "Can you ever find it in your heart to forgive me? Yours forever and forever, Lilly." Then she added a P. S.—"Congratulations on winning the lottery! Hope to see you soon."

Probably ol' Fred saw through the "tearstain" too! Agendas are often harder to hide than a rhinoceros on a roller coaster. And vibrant Christian leaders won't even try. They love sincerely—without a thought of return. Just like Jesus: "You see, at just the right time, when we were still powerless, Christ died for the ungodly" (Rom. 5:6). The only thing the Lord Jesus Christ gained by giving His life for us was our love. We were too poor to give Him anything else.

C. Puppies aren't concerned with pedigrees. People are concerned with pedigrees! When that caregiver walks through the front door, the puppy doesn't check his or her credentials. The puppy doesn't even care whether the caregiver has completed a course in puppy maintenance. The only thing that puppy cares about is caring.

Charismatic preacher T. D. Jakes said, "People in my generation are lost, hungry, in prison, wounded, and alone. Many are dying without knowing God—not dying for the lack of theology, but for lack of love."

Christian leaders must major in caring. Whether or not every "i" is dotted and every "t" is crossed in some plan or program is of little consequence in light of the eternal condition of a person's soul. You know the popular saying: People don't care how much you know as long as they know how much you care.

In December 1999 Reuters News Service reported that the E-mail service of computer giant Microsoft Corporation was temporarily disabled because the $600 billion corporation hadn't paid a $35 registration fee for its domain name. Many of its 50 million users were prevented from accessing their accounts.

But someone cared. A computer programmer in Tennessee discovered the oversight and paid the company that controls domain names. With his own credit card, the man bought back Microsoft's E-mail name and bailed out the giant corporation.

The investment was small—a little bit of caring—but the return benefited millions.

D. Puppies are loyal by nature. You don't have to send a puppy to loyalty school. Puppies will love you whether you feed them gourmet horse meat from designer cans or break open one of those oversized dog food bags from Sam's Club and dump some of its granulated contents onto an aluminum pie plate.

The Christian leader who leads people forward is loyal by nature. He or she is not *for you* today and *faulting* you tomorrow. That leader is with you for the long haul—through *mental thickness* and *performance thinness.*

Jesus, the greatest leader, could have yanked the WWJD bracelet off the apostle Peter's wrist after that fiasco around the fire when Peter denied knowing Him. Instead, He put an arm around his shoulder, forgave him, gave him an opportunity to ask forgiveness, and then presented him a ministry assignment: "Feed my sheep."

And you'd better believe that some of the best sheep-feeding in history took place after that wonderful incident! Loyalty breeds excellence.

There's a classic story of a Christian and a Jew who were in business together. Trying to eliminate any partisanship and to form some sort of spiritual consensus, they agreed to attend each other's place of worship. The Christian went with his Jewish partner to the synagogue and listened to the rabbi. As the offering plates were passed, the Christian glanced over to see that his partner had written a check for 10 percent of his part of the earnings that week and had placed it into the offering plate.

The following week, the Jewish partner attended church with the Christian and listened to the pastor. Again, the offering plates were passed. The Jewish business partner noticed as the Christian reached into his pocket, pulled out a dollar, and put it into the plate.

Struck with the dollar gift and remembering the offering he gave at the synagogue the previous week, the Jewish partner leaned over and whispered to his Christian partner, "A dollar? Almost thou persuadest me to be a Christian."

E. Puppies are enthusiastic about their work. You can be sadder than a one-term governor on a two-year probation and still perk up when you see a puppy. Puppies have a way of draining the "dreads" out of you. They enjoy their work—and everybody knows it.

A group of schoolchildren were invited to take time from the classroom and stand along the road as a vice presidential candidate's motorcade passed by. Their only instruction was to hold up some handmade political signs and cheer when the candidate drove by.

They did their job with great gusto. As a motorcade rounded the corner and headed toward their spot, they waved their placards and cheered at the top of their lungs. There was one slight problem, however: They had cheered for the wrong motorcade. But imagine how the folks in those funeral cars were encouraged when they drove by that enthusiastic group!

The influence of enthusiasm. A leader of people must be enthusiastic. The apostle Paul penned, "Whatever you do, work at it with all your heart" (Col. 3:23). Leighton Ford writes, "One gets the impression when reading about Jesus' disciples that, for all their blunders and shortcomings, they were with Him for the long haul."[4] Ford tells us of staff inscriptions written on the leather-bound volumes of speeches given by U.S. Securities and Exchange Commission Chairman Harold Williams and given to him at his retirement. Among their comments: "You gave meaning and significance throughout our professional lives." "Working with you was a fine form of post-graduate education." "Always it was fun! Thanks!" Ford comments, "The would-be leader in Jesus' style should ask not just 'Am I getting the job done?' but 'Am I fun to work with? Do I have a contagious enthusiasm?'"[5]

"People first" leadership is also seen in the lives of Early Church leaders.

2. The Barnabas benchmark

A benchmark is "something that serves as a standard by which others may be measured or judged."[6] Luke described an apostle named Barnabas: "He was a good man, full of the Holy Spirit and faith" (Acts 11:24). A Levite by genealogy and a native of Cyprus, Barnabas was probably one of the first converts to Christianity after Pentecost.

When it comes to putting people first, above plans and programs, Barnabas sets the standard. Barnabas's name means "son of prophecy," and his manner of ministry suggests that his words of prophecy were good words. But the apostles gave him a descriptive nickname: "son of encouragement." He had a special gift for influencing people by overlooking their worst and bringing out their best.

We know that he was a gospel teammate of the apostle Paul, who accompanied him on his missionary journeys. Beyond the historical account of his fruitful ministry, we know little. He seemed to drop from the New Testament landscape after his well-known debate with Paul in a church business meeting about not renewing John Mark's pastoral staff contract.

As is often the case, Barnabas's life and ministry is displayed in several benchmark incidents. And those incidents provide us with lasting and important insights into New Testament leadership.

A. Barnabas set a standard for generosity. He put the necessities of others above personal niceties: "Joseph, a Levite from Cyprus, whom the apostles called Barnabas (which means Son of Encouragement), sold a field he owned and brought the money and put it at the apostles' feet" (Acts 4:36-37). Barnabas perceived that the "real needs" of New Testament Christians were more important than his real estate holdings.

Leadership involves sacrifice. Often, personal plans and perks have to be put on hold to meet the immediate needs of fellow workers. In a not-so-complimentary account, *Sports Illustrated* magazine columnist Rick Reilly chronicled the life of a current "prince of perks," a professional baseball player:

> In the San Francisco Giants' clubhouse, everybody knows the score: 24-1. There are 24 teammates, and there's Barry Bonds. . . . There are 24 teammates who hang out with one another, play cards and bond, and there's Bonds, sequestered in the far corner of the clubhouse with his p.r. man, masseur, flex guy, weight trainer, three lockers, a reclining massage chair and a big-screen television that only he can see.[7]

The Master didn't have a massage chair, or a big-screen TV that only He could watch. He could have afforded it. After all, He owned everything. But He chose a borrowed manger, rented rooms, and a gratis gravesite to meet the eternal needs of others. "A student is not above his teacher, nor a servant above his master" (Matt. 10:24).

B. Barnabas set a standard for forgiveness. Following Paul's (then known as Saul) conversion and then his mentoring by Ananias, he began a preaching-and-teaching ministry that drew derisive questions and comments from the apostles.

"This man hasn't been to Bible college!"

"How can you trust your future to someone with a past like that?"

"He's not one of us—I bet he doesn't even know how to fish!"

"And besides, he threw Christians into jail and threw away the key!"

Barnabas took him in (Acts 9:26-28).

He had known mercy and grace at the hand of the Galilean. Jesus had made a trade with Barnabas: a robe of righteousness for a suit of filthy rags. Barnabas could never live a life of exclusivity again. He didn't know a lot about Saul/Paul's credentials, but he knew they shared the same Savior!

No Exceptions

Vibrant Christian leaders understand that God can use just about anyone in His service. An Internet contributor chronicled these facts and offered these comments:

Moses stuttered.

David's armor didn't fit.

Hosea's wife was a prostitute.

Jacob was a liar.

David had an affair.

Solomon was too rich.

Abraham was too old.

Jeremiah was depressed and suicidal.

Miriam was a gossip.

Elijah was burned out.

Martha was a worrywart.

Samson had long hair.

Lazarus was dead.

Sure—there are lots of reasons why God shouldn't want us. But if we are in love with Him, if we hunger for Him more than our next breath, He'll use us in spite of who we are, where we've been, or what we look like.[8]

Paul seconds the motion: "Accept one another, then, just as Christ accepted you, in order to bring praise to God" (Rom. 15:7).

C. Barnabas set the standard for encouragement. Barnabas lived up to his nickname. Acts 11:22-23 says, "News of this reached the ears of the church at Jerusalem, and they sent Barnabas to Antioch. When he arrived and saw the evidence of the grace of God, he was glad and encouraged them all to remain true to the Lord with all their hearts."

The New Testament leaders in Jerusalem are looking over their team roster. "Now, let's see—who do we have on the team who could go to Antioch to build up new Christians in the faith and encourage some burned-out Christian workers?"

Suddenly one of the leaders speaks up: "That's a no-brainer."

"Yeah, right," another chimes in. "Barnabas is our man!"

They knew Barnabas would mix cheer with his challenge. They knew the apostle's arms were strong enough to lift the discouraged and lighten the load of the drained. Encouragement was written on his countenance. Encouragement flowed from his speech. Encouragement was in his handshake.

Leadership without encouragement is like a milkshake without milk. There's no room for halfhearted leadership.

D. Barnabas set the standard for restoration. It was the "uncivil war" of the New Testament.

Some time later Paul said to Barnabas, "Let us go back and visit the brothers in all the towns where we preached the word of the Lord and see how they are doing." Barnabas wanted to take John, also called Mark, with them, but Paul did not think it wise to take him, because he had deserted them in Pamphylia and had not continued with them in the work. They had such a sharp disagreement that they parted company. Barnabas took Mark and sailed for Cyprus, but Paul chose Silas and left, commended by the brothers to the grace of the Lord. He went through Syria and Cilicia, strengthening the churches" *(Acts 15:36-41)*.

Over the years the altercation has gotten more coverage than an Ali-Frazier championship boxing bout. But it was really nothing more than Christians acting like humans. Not everybody has to have the same tennis shoe size or walk a mile in the same number of minutes to be on the same journey. Sure, Paul and Barnabas had a disagreement and a division, but two strong ministries survived— and eventually thrived—because they had the same mission statement. Paul took off his gospel boxing gloves and "went through Syria and Cilicia, strengthening the churches." He had enough spiritual strength left.

And Barnabas "sailed for Cyprus." Obviously, that first "church split" hadn't taken the wind out of everyone's sails! But the dynamics of the division deserve a second look.

"John Mark is a quitter," Paul contended. "He's not dependable, and he shouldn't be on the team."

Barnabas countered, "Now, Brother Paul, I know he struck out once, but that doesn't mean he's a quitter. He's had a pretty good batting average, and I think we ought to give him another trip to the plate."

Overlooked in the tabloid happenings was a young man with a bruised spirit who needed someone to bring a restoration out of the situation.

In the midst of congressional intern Chandra Levy's disappearance controversy in Washington, D.C., United States President George W. Bush was asked by a reporter at a news conference to comment. Adamantly, the president replied, "This isn't about 'Washington Whispers'—this is about someone's daughter who's missing!" In other words, we need to focus on search and rescue, not on saving face.

New Testament leadership focuses on search and rescue—on restoration. Someone needs another chance. Someone needs an opportunity to pour the cement of second effort over the soiled sands of his or her failure.

Second-Chance Savior

The greatest leader was always willing to give someone another trip to the plate—even if he or she had struck out before. "O Jerusalem, Jerusalem, you who kill the prophets and stone those sent to you, how often I have longed to gather your children together, as a hen gathers her chicks under her wings, but you were not willing" (Matt. 23:37).

Newspaper columnist Tom Erlich gave further insight in an article on genuine leadership authority:

Jesus listened. That is where true authority starts—in listening, both to the other person and to God. Jesus heard their voices and saw into their hearts. He treated their words as treasure, not as an occasion to demonstrate His own superiority. He treated their lives as treasure, not as an occasion to smother their uniqueness in order to build himself up. Jesus was a prophet in the Old Testament sense, namely, one who sees the present for what it is. We try to turn the Messiah into a fortune-teller, but His teachings had to do with handling reality: human sinfulness, relationships, God's love, decisions about wealth, and the reality of God's sin-breaking kingdom.[9]

There's another stirring example of the "people first" policy in the New Testament church.

3. The Macedonian model

"Modeling" simply means to exemplify excellence. Some New Testament churches might be known as "model churches." The apostle Paul gives us these words: "Now, brothers, we want you to know about the grace that God has given the Macedonian churches" (2 Cor. 8:1).

Those Early Church Christians remind us of the classic story of the egg farmer who took a volleyball into the hen house as an incentive for the layers to go beyond the call of duty. "Ladies, this is what the other hens are producing!" he announced to them.

The ministry and motivations of Macedonian Christians were larger than life. This country, located north of Greece, contained such well-known New Testament cities as Berea, Philippi, and Thessalonica and formed the backdrop for some of the apostle Paul's greatest ministry triumphs.

There was just something about those Macedonians! They knew how to put people first: they were devoted to one another.

A. They gave more than they had. "Out of the most severe trial, their overflowing joy and their extreme poverty welled up in rich generosity" (2 Cor. 8:2). Kicked about like political footballs, they always seemed to end up with a financial shortfall. But they had formed links of faith with the people of God that would not be broken by the events of time.

Something was more important to them than a 12-week seminar on spiritual gifts: they had an immediate and urgent need to share an offering with suffering Christians in Jerusalem.

They didn't have much of an investment in the stock market. Their mutual funds were lacking, but their mutual *concerns* were paying outstanding spiritual dividends.

B. They carried out ministry from a deficit position. New Testament leaders understand that they will often give from a deficit position. There may not be enough training. Their gifts survey may indicate a need to be put into "righteous receivership." There may not be enough funds to start a mission for homeless mosquitoes. But a heart willing to give its resources to another has the promise of heaven's hand. "Give, and it will be given to you. A good measure, pressed down, shaken together and running over, will be poured into your lap. For with the measure you use, it will be measured to you" (Luke 6:38).

C. They were joyful in their duties. "I testify that they gave as much as they were able, and even beyond their ability. Entirely on their own, they urgently pleaded with us for the privilege of sharing in this service to the saints" (2 Cor. 8:3-4). The Macedonian churches didn't have dues—there was no entry fee for their faith. They considered personal sacrifice for the supply of another a privilege. They took joy in their ministry to others—they were devoted to one another.

D. The missing leadership link. Joy is the missing link in the lives of many leaders. For too long they have been trying to pay their "dos" with ministry credit cards that have reached their maximum limits without realizing any emotional return. To give of oneself for the benefit of another out of pure joy is a religious rarity. Not so with the Macedonian Christians: They begged to be a blessing! Can you imagine your church ushers walking down the center aisle and having people jump up from their pew to stop them: "Please don't forget our row, usher!" Let that happen once or twice, and your church will have to place a heart defibrillator in the foyer!

But isn't joy the true call of New Testament leadership? Consider these Scripture verses:

- "The kingdom of heaven is like treasure hidden in a field. When a man found it, he hid it again, and then in his *joy* went and sold all he had and bought that field" (Matt. 13:44, emphasis added).

- "But the angel said to them, 'Do not be afraid. I bring you good news of great *joy* that will be for all the people'" (Luke 2:10, emphasis added).

- "Until now you have not asked for anything in my name. Ask and you will receive, and your *joy* will be complete" (John 16:24, emphasis added).

- "The disciples were filled with *joy* and with the Holy Spirit" (Acts 13:52, emphasis added).

- "May the God of hope fill you with all *joy* and peace as you trust in him, so that you may overflow with hope by the power of the Holy Spirit" (Rom. 15:13, emphasis added).

- "I have great confidence in you; I take great pride in you. I am greatly encouraged; in all our troubles my *joy* knows no bounds" (2 Cor. 7:4, emphasis added).
- "In all my prayers for all of you, I always pray with *joy*" (Phil. 1:4, emphasis added).
- "Obey your leaders and submit to their authority. They keep watch over you as men who must give an account. Obey them so that their work will be a *joy,* not a burden, for that would be of no advantage to you" (Heb. 13:17, emphasis added).
- "Though you have not seen him, you love him; and even though you do not see him now, you believe in him and are filled with an inexpressible and glorious *joy*" (1 Pet. 1:8, emphasis added).
- "I have much to write to you, but I do not want to use paper and ink. Instead, I hope to visit you and talk with you face to face, so that our *joy* may be complete" (2 John 12, emphasis added).
- "To him who is able to keep you from falling and to present you before his glorious presence without fault and with great *joy*" (Jude 24, emphasis added).

E. Their sanctification was reflected in their obedience. "They did not do as we expected, but they gave themselves first to the Lord and then to us in keeping with God's will" (2 Cor. 8:5).

Macedonian Christians were able to give everything they had, because they were used to holding nothing back. Everything belonged to the Lord—including their lives. Paul wrote about that in his call to the church at Rome: "I urge you, brothers, in view of God's mercy, to offer your bodies as living sacrifices, holy and pleasing to God—this is your spiritual act of worship" (Rom. 12:1).

Every Christian leader can say, "They did not do as we expected." But few can say, "They gave themselves first to the Lord and then to us in keeping with God's will." The difference between the two is the difference between abundance and redundancy. One dwells on the level of mediocrity—*contentment in doing the same boring motions to their swan song*—while the other seeks higher ground and subsequently struggles to bring in filled nets from the right side of the boat.

Three successful adult sons decided they would do something special for their elderly mother on Mother's Day. After all the sacrifices their mother had made, they reasoned that with their wealth they could make the day memorable. They got together over lunch and decided on their gifts.

"I'll move her into a brand-new home," one said. "I have just the home in mind. It's in an upscale subdivision I just built—a five-bedroom home with four baths and a three-car garage."

"She'll love it!" one of the sons offered.

The second son made his commitment: "I'll give her a brand-new car from one of my Lexus dealerships."

The third son racked his brain to try to top the gifts of his brothers. Finally, he decided on giving his mother a rare South American bird from his personal collection. It was known to be the only one in captivity.

Mother's Day arrived, and the proud sons made their presentations to their beloved mother. Several weeks later, Mom wrote interesting letters to each of her sons.

To the son who moved her into a new home, she wrote, "What a thoughtful gift! I love my new home, but I'll have to say I feel a little lost in here. The other night I went to the kitchen in the middle of the night to get a drink of water, and it took me 15 minutes to find my way back to my room. There sure are a lot of rooms!"

To the car dealer son, she wrote, "Son, I sure do enjoy that new car you gave me. Every day I go out to the garage and sit in it. I only wish that I had renewed my driver's license. I would have enjoyed driving it out on the road."

"Son, your gift was the most practical of all," she wrote to the third son, who had given the rare bird from his luxurious collection. "I shared it with my friends. The ladies of my missionary society came over last Saturday for the nicest barbecue. They said to tell you that was the best chicken they ever ate!"

For that rare bird, the gift was in the sacrifice.

Sanctification (setting oneself apart for holy use) was modeled by the Son of God. "For them I sanctify myself, that they too may be truly sanctified" (John 17:19). Calvary was the ultimate act of service. Jesus "humbled himself and became obedient to death—even death on a cross!" (Phil. 2:8). "Even" is an astounding word—one that signifies the depths and heights to which the Savior would go to meet the needs of others.

New Testament leaders know that true service begins at the altar of sacrifice, not on the throne of authority.

It's said that a farmer placed a classified ad in the "Personals" section of the newspaper: "Lonely farmer on 1,000-acre farm seeks wife with tractor. Please send photo of tractor with reply."

New Testament leadership isn't about tractors. It's about people—people for whom Jesus died. Our job is to do more than manipulate the dials on organizational machinery that will be obsolete far too soon. Our job is to minister to people—to find them, lead them to the Savior, train them, and then to send them out to start the process all over again.

People first!

1 DISCOVERING THE TRIUMPHS OF TEAMWORK

A NERVOUS ECONOMIST ONCE SAID, "The quickest way to double your money is to fold it over and put it back into your pocket." That may or may not be a proven financial principle, but in Christian leadership circles, the best way to double your *productivity and influence* is by teaming up with others. One Super Bowl-winning coach answered the curious questions of a reporter about his great success—"I'm an ordinary guy surrounded by extraordinary men."

Business consultant and training specialist for Fortune 500 companies Brian Molitor defined a team: "A team is two or more people who are prepared, equipped, and committed to working together to achieve a common purpose. It may be a family, school system, department, congregation, or corporation."[1]

New Testament leaders discovered the triumphs of teamwork early on. The apostle Paul had joined forces with a husband-and-wife team, Aquila and Priscilla, religious refugees from Rome who were exiled because of their national origin. Their mutual love for the Lord and their mutual tent-making careers instantly solidified the relationship between the veteran missionary and the talented new converts.

Later, the couple accompanied Paul on a missionary journey and served as "Bible teachers" in Ephesus. Their tireless efforts in spreading the Christian faith saw them eventually returning in triumph to Rome, where they established a New Testament house church.

Prominent leaders for a time, they gave self-effacing service that's seen in at least one defining episode.

> After spending some time in Antioch, Paul set out from there and traveled from place to place throughout the region of Galatia and Phrygia, strengthening all the disciples.
>
> Meanwhile a Jew named Apollos, a native of Alexandria, came to Ephesus. He was a learned man, with a thorough knowledge

of the Scriptures. He had been instructed in the way of the Lord, and he spoke with great fervor and taught about Jesus accurately, though he knew only the baptism of John. He began to speak boldly in the synagogue. When Priscilla and Aquila heard him, they invited him to their home and explained to him the way of God more adequately.

When Apollos wanted to go to Achaia, the brothers encouraged him and wrote to the disciples there to welcome him. On arriving, he was a great help to those who by grace had believed. For he vigorously refuted the Jews in public debate, proving from the Scriptures that Jesus was the Christ *(Acts 18:23-28)*.

Influential leaders in the Christian community at Ephesus, Acquila and Priscilla had a heart for ministry teamwork. They immediately spotted a potentially valuable member of the team, a Jew from Alexandria named Apollos. Not only was he a bright scholar, but as is seen in his later life and ministry, he had great charisma.

Instead of being intimidated by this rising star, Aquila and Priscilla saw an opportunity to utilize his strengths in carrying out the objectives in their statement of purpose.

He was familiar with the Law and the Prophets, but he lacked understanding in the way of Christ. The consecrated couple immediately began a mentoring process that resulted in Apollos's Christian education.

What do you do with people who obviously have equal or greater ministry strengths than yours? The New Testament Church shows us. First, you thank the Lord for them! Then you . . .

Encourage them.

Train them.

Use them.

Endorse them.

Support them.

Such persons have the potential for helping you reach your own ministry goals.

Apollos was a member of the team. And when he succeeded, every New Testament leader moved up a notch. 1 Cor. 12:21-26 teaches us about this marvelous interdependence:

The eye cannot say to the hand, "I don't need you!" And the head cannot say to the feet, "I don't need you!" On the contrary, those parts of the body that seem to be weaker are indispensable, and the parts that we think are less honorable we treat with special honor. And the parts that are unpresentable are treated with special modesty, while our presentable parts need no special treatment. But God has combined the members of the body and has given greater honor to the parts that lacked it, so that there should be no division in the body, but that its parts should have equal concern for each other. If one part suffers, every part suffers with it; if one part is honored, every part rejoices with it.

There's a Leader in the House

If you need immediate medical attention, you might ask, "Is there a doctor in the house?" But if you need support staff to carry out your church or organization's mission, you might ask, "Is there a future leader in the house?"

"Yes!" is God's final answer.

There's a leader in every church congregation. The Spirit of the living God has already taken care of the situation. Read on:

To each one of us grace has been given as Christ apportioned it. This is why it says: "When he ascended on high, he led captives in his train and gave gifts to men." (What does "he ascended" mean except that he also descended to the lower, earthly regions? He who descended is the very one who ascended higher than all the heavens, in order to fill the whole universe.) It was he who gave some to be apostles, some to be prophets, some to be evangelists, and some to be pastors and teachers, to prepare God's people for works of service, so that the body of Christ may be built up *(Eph. 4:7-12)*.

God has all the gifts in place. Now all He needs is for someone to recognize and release them for the benefit of the Body. In fact, those gifts may be combined into a powerful and effective team. Smith and Lindsay say in *Leading Change in Your World*, "Teamwork is the result of individuals working together in a spirit of agreement and unity to accomplish a shared vision and organizational objectives. Often teams enable ordinary people to accomplish extraordinary results."[2]

There's a classic story of a church in which the preacher and the choir director weren't getting along. Soon the tumult began to influ-ence the worship service—especially during the choral response at the end of the sermon.

For five miserable weeks the "worship war" waged on.

The first week, the preacher gave a stirring message on the need to give oneself in service to the Lord. The choir director answered by having the choir sing "I Shall Not Be Moved."

The next week, the preacher came back with a sermon on tithing, and the choir ended the service with "Jesus Paid It All."

The third week, the preacher's ire was beginning to build. He preached a scathing message on the evils of gossip in the church. With delight, the choir director had the choir stand and sing "I Love to Tell the Story."

The warfare continued. The preacher couldn't help but com-ment on the goings-on, and finally, at the end of his sermon on the fourth week, he expressed the fact that he was considering his resig-nation. Imagine his dismay when the choir ended the service with the song "Oh, Why Not Tonight?"

The preacher finally surrendered. At the end of the fifth week's sermon, he told the church that Jesus was leading him away from that church. Beaming, the choir director had the choir stand and sing "What a Friend We Have in Jesus."

The choir itself is a prime example of powerful teamwork (even when the purpose is not so pious).

Individually, some of the choir members may have the vocal ability of a tree frog with laryngitis. But the croaking of the one is *usually* lost in the sounds of the combined voices in the choir. The vocal abilities of another make up for the weaknesses of the one.

The New Testament is filled with the triumphs of teamwork. In particular, the Acts of the Apostles gives us leadership insights, not just in theory but also in practice.

TIPS FOR WORKING WITH MINISTRY TEAMS

Brian Molitor also says there are basic ingredients for a team's success:

1. Clear purpose and direction
2. Effective leadership

3. Productive interpersonal relations
4. Communication/listening skills
5. Problem-solving and decision-making skills
6. Trust
7. Conflict resolution methods
8. Proper skills, knowledge, and abilities
9. Sufficient resources, information, supplies, and equipment
10. Fair performance evaluation, recognition, and reward systems[3]

With those ingredients in mind, whether you need a team of 2, 20, or 200, here are some principles from the first-century front lines that will help you put it together:

1. Find them

Good lay ministry teams start with good team members. They don't usually advertise in the classified section, and they're seldom illuminated in the glow of blue lights at Kmart in a two-for-one special. In fact, good workers are usually hard to find. While the military and industry use recruiters to find personnel, the new millennium church often has to deploy "beggars."

Not so with the Early Church. It had a dilemma. It also needed personnel. One of its star players, Judas, had a terrible accident on the playing field and was permanently sidelined. And it made such an impact on the crowd that they even renamed the stadium in memory of the incident (Acts 1:15-20). Judas needed to be replaced.

The apostle Peter was chairman of the search committee. Some of the steps they took in the process offer us some insights into lay ministry team recruitment.

A. Start with a good direction. Author and denominational leader Earle L. Wilson tells of speaking at a conference in a lakeside retreat center. After the afternoon recreation break, one of the conferees expressed frustration to the speaker about their canoeing expedition. He explained that once his canoeing buddy and he pushed off from the dock, they couldn't seem to make any progress.

Dr. Wilson then asked a discerning question to the first-time canoeists, "How were you positioned in the canoe?"

The "sailors" gave an interesting reply. "We were sitting in the canoe facing each other."

The problem was solved—they weren't getting anywhere because they were going in opposite directions![4]

Direction is important, especially in Christian leadership. To attract good team members, they need to see that their potential leader is going somewhere. The laity must have confidence in their leader. And likewise, the leader must have enough confidence in the laity to delegate assignments and authority to them. In one of his earlier works, Christian pollster George Barna wrote, "I found that the leaders of the growing churches delegated responsibility without anxiety. It seemed that those pastors perceived delegation as a means to an end; it was a way to empower other people to do ministry."[5] Jump forward 10 years, and the need for lay leaders is still there. But sadly, as Barna observes in one of his latest studies, "Only 2 percent of Protestant senior pastors name personal or lay leadership development, vision clarification and vision communication or strategic development of the ministry as top ministry priorities."[6]

The apostle Peter had a lay leadership development direction. He had left the fading embers of apostasy, where he had denied his Lord around a campfire, and had begun a new life, one with new resolve: to put the programs and purpose of Christ first in his life.

God's Word, not his emotions, was now his five-star standard for recruitment.

> In those days Peter stood up among the believers (a group numbering about a hundred and twenty) and said, "Brothers, the Scripture had to be fulfilled which the Holy Spirit spoke long ago through the mouth of David concerning Judas, who served as guide for those who arrested Jesus—he was one of our number and shared in this ministry."
>
> (With the reward he got for his wickedness, Judas bought a field; there he fell headlong, his body burst open and all his intestines spilled out. Everyone in Jerusalem heard about this, so they called that field in their language Akeldama, that is, Field of Blood.)
>
> "For," said Peter, "it is written in the book of Psalms, 'May his place be deserted; let there be no one to dwell in it,' and, 'May another take his place of leadership'" (Acts 1:15-20).

"It is written." Peter was saying, "We need to rebuild the team, and we're going to do it by the Book." A God-directed purpose is a prerequisite for building a lay ministry team.

Really, it's the difference between *flooding* and the *flow* of a river. With flooding, the potential power of water currents is out of control, wandering aimlessly (and most often dangerously) across the land. They need direction and purpose. The wisdom writer summed it up, "Where there is no vision, the people perish" (Prov. 29:18, KJV).

But a river that is flowing within its banks has direction and purpose. It is useful. It can be channeled. It can be a source of refreshment. It can carry people along to a certain destination.

What's the purpose of your church or organization? Evangelism? Discipleship? Stewardship? Education? Fellowship? Worship? Probably all of the above. And when those "streams" are combined within the banks of a stated purpose, a common commitment to Christlikeness, and a common dependency on the power of the Holy Spirit, the Kingdom truly keeps moving ahead.

Flooding scatters. *Flow* gathers.

B. Take a good look around you. Gary McIntosh wrote, "One of the trends clearly on the horizon is the move from a 'Pastor is King' approach to a 'Collaborative Team' approach to ministry."[7]

An airline industry recruiter needed three more pilots to meet his quota for the year. He decided to conduct an open house at the local airport. It wasn't long into the gathering before the recruiter spotted two young men lingering beside one of the planes.

They certainly looked the part. They were interested. They had bright faces. They were muscular. They were well dressed. The recruiter introduced himself. "Gentlemen, I'm Mr. Needmore. I just happened to notice how interested you seem to be in this plane. Do you have an interest in flying?"

"I sure do!" one of the young men replied excitedly.

The other young man added, "He sure does! He's a pilot, and I'm his brother."

The representative shook their hands and continued with enthusiasm at the thought of gaining a recruit. "A pilot? I can surely use him! And what do you do?" He said to the other brother.

The brother answered, "I'm a woodchopper."

"A woodchopper?" The recruiter said with a puzzled look. "I'm afraid we don't need any woodchoppers right now."

The pilot brother broke in emphatically, "Well, if you don't need him, you don't need me! We're a team. He chops the wood and I *pile it!*"

Christian recruiter, take a look around you. Some of your best workers may already be "piling" and "chopping." The apostle Peter gave us a hint: "Therefore it is necessary to choose one of the men who have been with us the whole time the Lord Jesus went in and out among us, beginning from John's baptism to the time when Jesus was taken up from us. For one of these must become a witness with us of his resurrection" (Acts 1:21-22).

"Before we start an ad campaign, we'd better see if there's anyone already in the camp who may have the qualifications we need," the chairman of the search committee seemed to be saying. That's good advice. Some of your best team members have been with you the longest (or in some cases, the shortest). Good recruiting begins right where you are.

- State the need (along with the qualifications) in your publications.
- Do a spiritual gifts inventory during a worship service.
- Start a training class for Christian workers.
- Notice those in your place of ministry who seem to possess needed skills.
- Encourage the giftedness of ministry standouts.
- Don't overlook the younger in search of the older.
- Observe faithfulness and zeal.
- Start a mentoring program.
- Ask for referrals.

Church leader and on-line columnist Misael Zaragoza said, "Ultimately, your success lies within your ability to recognize and recruit potential leaders for your church. The better you are at surrounding yourself with people of high potential, the greater your chance for potential success." He then gives some characteristics for "spotting the 'eagles'"—

People with leadership potential
Make things happen. . . .
Influence others. . . .
Add value to you. . . .
Possess a great attitude. . . .
Provide ideas that help the church. . . .

Live up to their commitments. . . .

Display loyalty.[8]

C. Ask the Holy Spirit to guide you. The third person of the Trinity is committed to being our "should" or "shouldn't" Guide (John 16:13). The pathways of ministry are dotted with the "walking wounded" who ignored the still, small voice of the Spirit and listened to the noisy demands of the crowd. What took Early Church leaders 40 days of fasting and prayer to decide, new millennium leaders often settle in 40 seconds! The focus of the search committee was on earnest prayer:

> So they proposed two men: Joseph called Barsabbas (also known as Justus) and Matthias. Then they prayed, "Lord, you know everyone's heart. Show us which of these two you have chosen to take over this apostolic ministry, which Judas left to go where he belongs." Then they cast lots, and the lot fell to Matthias; so he was added to the eleven apostles (*Acts 1:23-26*).

Of course, their actions were more than a "roll of the dice." They were carrying out a very important and sacred tradition of seeking the Lord's direction through the choosing by lots.

2. Feed them

Lay ministry team members need help. "Many are called but a few are *frozen*," the well-known tongue-in-cheek saying implies. The "chosen are frozen" in many cases simply because they don't know what to do! They're like the guy in the TV commercial who's working in a medical research lab. When he's addressed as "Doctor," he responds, "I'm not a doctor—but I did stay at Holiday Inn Express last night!" The implication is that he was alert enough to be a medical researcher because he had a good night's rest in a comfortable motel. We know, however, that he didn't necessarily have good *qualifications* just because he had good *accommodations*.

It's the same in Christian ministry. Christians aren't qualified for service simply because they sit in the services! They need to be assisted—they need training. They need a facilitator, a leader who will help them become their best for God.

In an August 2001 Crosswalk.com column on "Workplace in the Near Future," Cathie Cowie looked into the 2005 leadership environment: "In every new work culture lifelong learning will be a requirement. Performance improvement will be a constant focus and it will parallel all knowledge tracks in training. Team development and team skills will be a major necessary competency."[9]

Christian laypersons in Antioch needed a feeding. They were suffering from a deficiency in their spiritual diet. "Old school" teachers were trying to convince them to mix the fried chicken of their new faith with the manna of the old Mosaic Law. Two "teacher's aides" were given the assignment to assist veteran instructors Paul and Barnabas in righting some doctrinal wrongs among the Gentile converts (see Acts 15:22-29). Notice the care and feeding of the Gentile Christians.

A. They taught them with authority. There wasn't any wiggle room when it came to preaching and teaching the doctrines of the Christian faith. This wasn't an assignment for someone who would overlook the inequities of these new Christians. This wasn't a job for a rookie with a weak handshake and a soft sell. This was a job for soldiers who had a few stripes and combat medals on their uniforms—who would be willing to proclaim, "Thus saith the Lord," without blushing.

The apostles and elders knew that a bad start would result in a disastrous ending. From the beginning, the Antioch Christians had to know what was expected of them. The choice was made (Acts 15:22): "Then the apostles and elders, with the whole church, decided to choose some of their own men and send them to Antioch with Paul and Barnabas. They chose Judas (called Barsabbas) and Silas, two men who were leaders among the brothers."

Notice, "two men who were *leaders* among the brothers" (emphasis added). Their *authority* came from their *authenticity*. A classroom and a teacher's quarterly do not a teacher make! The best teachers are those who have proven themselves first as followers—those who have spent more time "practicing" than "preaching." Successful Christian businessman Max DePree says that a Christian organization must live up to its promises: "There's a direct connection between who we claim to be and our accountability for that claim."[10]

Judas and Silas had the respect of the apostles and elders. They knew that the potential leaders in the church at Antioch would need to be men and women of authenticity.

Vibrant Christian leaders know that weak assignments result in tepid accomplishments.

- The commitment must be included in the job description.
- The assignment must be clearly communicated.
- The chain of command must be fully explained.
- The dimensions and timelines of the assignment must be established.
- The job expectations must not be assumed—they must be carefully spelled out.

B. They taught them with compassion. The teaching crew knew they weren't in Antioch to adjust the electrical circuits on righteous robots. These were flesh-and-blood Christians. They had abandoned the world to follow in the way of the Cross. The soil of their soul was freshly plowed. They didn't need to stomp seeds into it!

It was tough love with a tear in its eye (Acts 15:23-24): "With them they sent the following letter: The apostles and elders, your brothers, To the Gentile believers in Antioch, Syria and Cilicia: Greetings. We have heard that some went out from us without our authorization and disturbed you, troubling your minds by what they said."

The apostles and elders took the pressure off the new converts and potential leaders: "Your brothers." Instead of keeping them at an arm's length, they wrapped their arms around them. New Testament leaders are Christ-copiers. They learn compassion from the parable of the great shepherd who searched for one lost sheep (Luke 15). He showed patience and restraint with dumb sheep that didn't go where they were supposed to go. The great shepherd, of course, is Jesus.

1. He went to them—to where they were. Compassionate team leaders fill the caverns of ignorance with knowledge. They trade their skills for the inexperience of their charges. They begin at level one. They don't overlook the details and don't assume that other people know how to lead. They tell them how to lead.

2. He lifted them up—he added his strength to their weakness. Compassionate team leaders take up the slack. They do the extra praying for a while. They take the first steps in encouraging and affirming. They show by their example how to do the job right.

3. He brought them home—from where they were to where they ought to be. Compassionate team leaders know that the teaching process is not complete until someone has learned. Effort after effort. Time after time. Word upon word. Great teachers never give up. (Obviously, none of us would be here if they had.)

And once they're home, the great shepherd stands guard over them with his very life. New Testament leadership is also quick to defend its followers. Once the followers know their captain isn't going to abandon them at the first whim or whine of another, they'll be strengthened to stick with him or her.

C. They taught them with simplicity. "So we all agreed to choose some men and send them to you with our dear friends Barnabas and Paul—men who have risked their lives for the name of our Lord Jesus Christ. Therefore we are sending Judas and Silas to confirm by word of mouth what we are writing" (Acts 15:25-27).

This wasn't about wall charts and diagrammed sentences. This wasn't about ministry manuals that would take a magna cum laude to read aloud. This was all about "show and tell." This was kindergarten-level training for kindergarten-level Christians.

You've heard the illustration. Vince Lombardi, the short Hall of Fame coach of the Green Bay Packers, would always begin his football training camps each year by holding up a football to those behemoths in sweats and cleats, saying, "Gentlemen, this is a football."

That's a good place to start. "Gentleman and ladies, this is a Sunday School class." "This is a committee." "This is a small group." "This is an offering plate." "This is a praise team." "This is a computer."

And proceed from there—slowly, deliberately, painstakingly—until everyone knows for sure what he or she is supposed to do.

They taught them lovingly. No harsh rebukes here. No "You oughta know better." Just loving concern for a people who needed to be taught how to be better servants of Christ. "It seemed good to the Holy Spirit and to us not to burden you with anything beyond the following requirements: You are to abstain from food sacrificed to idols, from blood, from the meat of strangled animals and from sexual immorality. You will do well to avoid these things" (Acts 15:28-29).

3. Form them.

"Breaking news." The television program was interrupted to a news cutaway. In San Antonio a man was trapped in his van by raging floodwaters. Seen with their life preserver vests strapped to them were several members of the water rescue team. Arm in arm, inch by inch—each depending on the other for sure footing—four team members made their way to the anxious man. Their strength was in their teamwork, their link to each other. Alone, a rescuer would have been swept away by the fast moving current. But together there was an opportunity to save a man who would be lost.

Soon the team reached the stranded man. And the process was reversed—this time including the victim—back to safety. The beauty of the rescue was in the individuals' working together. Isn't it the same for the Church? Our strength is in our teamwork!

Old Testament prophet Amos asked an interesting question: "Do two walk together unless they have agreed to do so?" (Amos 3:3). The context, of course, is the holy alignment of God's promises and God's judgment—carried out perfectly in the life of Israel. But it's an interesting leadership question as well. Can two walk (or work) together unless they are in agreement? Forming ministry teams is one of the great challenges of New Testament leadership. Misaligned teams (whether they're workers in the office or singers in the choir) can be an ecclesiastical volcano waiting to erupt.

In their August 2001 on-line leadership newsletter, Nelson Searcy, Jimmy Britt, and Kwan Ihn talked about working with teams: "As a team leader you can be your best when you remember to lead people, manage tasks, and facilitate decisions. Be conscientious about the different personality style within the group, and match your leadership tactics to the stage of team development."[11]

It's one of the most stirring scenes in the Acts of the Apostles. Paul gives a farewell speech that would be the envy of any itinerant evangelist who ever bid adieu on the last night of a revival crusade. But it's also a great commentary on the mentor-mentored relationship:

> And now, compelled by the Spirit, I am going to Jerusalem, not knowing what will happen to me there. I only know that in every city the Holy Spirit warns me that prison and hardships are facing me. However, I consider my life worth nothing to me, if only I may finish the race and complete the task the Lord Jesus has given me—the task of testifying to the gospel of God's grace.
>
> Now I know that none of you among whom I have gone about preaching the kingdom will ever see me again. Therefore, I declare to you today that I am innocent of the blood of all men. For I have not hesitated to proclaim to you the whole will of God. Keep watch over yourselves and all the flock of which the Holy Spirit has made you overseers. Be shepherds of the church

of God, which he bought with his own blood. I know that after I leave, savage wolves will come in among you and will not spare the flock. Even from your own number men will arise and distort the truth in order to draw away disciples after them. So be on your guard! Remember that for three years I never stopped warning each of you night and day with tears.

Now I commit you to God and to the word of his grace, which can build you up and give you an inheritance among all those who are sanctified. I have not coveted anyone's silver or gold or clothing. You yourselves know that these hands of mine have supplied my own needs and the needs of my companions. In everything I did, I showed you that by this kind of hard work we must help the weak, remembering the words the Lord Jesus himself said: "It is more blessed to give than to receive."

When he had said this, he knelt down with all of them and prayed. They all wept as they embraced him and kissed him. What grieved them most was his statement that they would never see his face again. Then they accompanied him to the ship (Acts 20:22-38).

Note that the response of the team to the farewell of its leader was grief! That's a mark of New Testament leadership: It leaves people grateful for encountering it.

On another occasion Barnabas, the encourager, made his way to Antioch to build a ministry team. The church had seen phenomenal growth, so the need for leaders was crucial. Acts 11:21-22 states, "The Lord's hand was with them, and a great number of people believed and turned to the Lord. News of this reached the ears of the church at Jerusalem, and they sent Barnabas to Antioch." His actions and attitudes recorded in Acts 11 give all of us some team-building tips.

A. He focused on the team's spiritual growth. Christian leaders are not just instructors. They are pastors as well. "When he arrived and saw the evidence of the grace of God, he was glad and encouraged them all to remain true to the Lord with all their hearts" (v. 23). Beginning where they were ("he arrived and saw the evidence of the grace of God"), Barnabas encouraged the new Christians to keep growing.

Any effort to spur the spiritual growth of Christian workers is time *more* than well spent! Gary McIntosh wrote, "Leaders in the

21st century are not simply managers of church programs. They are leaders of movements that help people on spiritual journeys find spiritual meaning."[12] Paul encouraged young Pastor Timothy to "fan into flame the gift of God" (2 Tim. 1:6). Ministry teams who are growing inwardly (in their spirits) as well as outwardly (in their skills) are teams who are growing in their effectiveness.

But that takes focus. For example, the sports coach doesn't *assume* the growth of the team—he or she *advances* it. Instruction is systematically given. Discipline is constructively enforced. Public affirmation is lavishly given.

It's the same for the ministry team. The leader creates the spiritual life drills:

- Start team meetings with the Word (systematic Bible study).
- Take time to pray (for each other and for others).
- Check spiritual progress (stress accountability).
- Offer spiritual retreats (get away).
- Take the team on instructional and inspirational outings.

Spiritual emphasis is the oil that makes organizational machinery run smoother. Neglect it, and friction is a given. Stress it, and friction will *still be a given!* (Don't forget that these are humans we're working with.) But the friction will be far less.

B. He linked the weaker team members to the stronger. Barnabas himself needed backup. He knew that another member of his home team had strengths that were needed for the project. "Then Barnabas went to Tarsus to look for Saul, and when he found him, he brought him to Antioch" (Acts 11:25-26). Saul/Paul was a "chosen vessel" (Acts 9:15, KJV).

One effective way to train leadership is through apprenticeship —linking beginners with veterans. Jesus himself learned carpentry by the skillful example of Joseph. Leadership skills are often like a cold: Stay in the room long enough with someone who has them, and soon you'll be "infected" with them.

C. He made a long-range training commitment to the team. "For a whole year Barnabas and Saul met with the church and taught great numbers of people. The disciples were called Christians first at Antioch" (Acts 11:26). The tenure paid off in a triumph: the disciples were called "Christians." The followers of *religion* became followers of *Christ!*

Forming a team takes time. One pizza party does not make a team. Over weeks and months and years, individuals start thinking alike and working together.

D. He expected advancement to come out of the team's adversities. Adversity is to be expected. Remember Paul's farewell speech? Here's the introduction: "And now, compelled by the Spirit, I am going to Jerusalem, not knowing what will happen to me there. I only know that in every city the Holy Spirit warns me that prison and hardships are facing me" (Acts 20:22-23).

He probably should have started with a humorous story! Why didn't he? Because "sticks and stones" go with the leadership territory. But every Christian leader can look back on those times of adversity—some happening before the ink had dried on their college diploma—and see that advancement resulted. (If nothing else, they improved our prayer life!)

Team trainees need to understand that they're a long way from the retirement watch. And along the way will be some uncertainties, some "prisons" and "hardships." But the advancement is worth the adversity: "I consider my life worth nothing to me, if only I may finish the race and complete the task the Lord Jesus has given me" (v. 24).

E. He expected the best out of the teams. And he wasn't disappointed. Acts 11:27-30 states:

> During this time some prophets came down from Jerusalem to Antioch. One of them, named Agabus, stood up and through the Spirit predicted that a severe famine would spread over the entire Roman world. (This happened during the reign of Claudius.) The disciples, each according to his ability, decided to provide help for the brothers living in Judea. This they did, sending their gift to the elders by Barnabas and Saul.

He allowed the new Christians time to adjust to each other and to their task. He gave them space for ministry trial and error. And then he simply expected them to run the plays!

Three friends were discussing their funeral services. "What do you want them to say about you when you're stretched out there in your casket?"

One of the friends answered, "I want them to say I was a good husband, father, and worker."

They turned to their friend. "And what do you want them to say about you?"

His answer startled them: "I want them to say, 'Look—he's moving!'"

4. Follow them

One cowpoke philosopher said, "If you're ridin' ahead of the herd, take a look back every now and then to make sure it's still there."

On another leg of his missionary journeys, the apostle Paul left an extended ministry stay in Corinth and circled back to Antioch. That "circling back" is another quality of New Testament leadership.

> Paul stayed on in Corinth for some time. Then he left the brothers and sailed for Syria, accompanied by Priscilla and Aquila. Before he sailed, he had his hair cut off at Cenchrea because of a vow he had taken. They arrived at Ephesus, where Paul left Priscilla and Aquila. He himself went into the synagogue and reasoned with the Jews. When they asked him to spend more time with them, he declined. But as he left, he promised, "I will come back if it is God's will." Then he set sail from Ephesus. When he landed at Caesarea, he went up and greeted the church and then went down to Antioch.
>
> After spending some time in Antioch, Paul set out from there and traveled from place to place throughout the region of Galatia and Phrygia, strengthening all the disciples *(Acts 18:18-23)*.

Quality control is a vital task of vibrant Christian leadership. It's one thing to birth the team; it's another to raise it!

And raising takes nurturing and supervision. It takes "following" as well as "leading."

You've seen "following" at your favorite restaurant. First, the server trainee "follows." For an appointed time, the new waiter or waitress simply follows the veteran server around. Table to table, often doing nothing more than standing there with a smile on his or her face, the trainee observes the proper way to wait on customers.

On one momentous day for the trainee, the role is reversed. The trainee takes control of the pen and notepad and makes his or her way around the table circuit. But guess who's right behind? That's right— the veteran. Now "following" takes on a whole new dimension.

The veteran follows the new server, staying a few steps back, to observe whether or not the customer is being served in a manner worthy of the restaurant's name.

Sometimes the veteran steps in to make up for a missed cue. And sometimes the veteran has to cover—to replace the new server because of an illness or absence.

Paul was a "follower." Sure, he would rather be preaching on the front lines in the synagogue. But he knew he had to spend some high-quality control time in the barracks, encouraging and instructing the troops toward excellence.

- He wanted to be sure they were doing their job according to their training.
- He wanted to make them aware of the latest methods.
- He wanted to see if they were getting along with the other workers.
- He wanted to be sure there weren't any personal problems impeding their work.
- He wanted them to know he truly cared about them.
- He wanted to let them know that he was available.

He was a faithful "follower." Yet "following" is becoming a rarity. George Barna wrote, "Most churches do not have any objective or regular process for evaluating how well their ministry is faring in any given dimension of ministry."[13]

The next step in putting a lay ministry team together . . .

5. Fire them

Of course, "firing" doesn't mean handing out "pink slips." It means motivating them. Brother Zeke went to the altar Sunday after Sunday, revival after revival, Friend Day after Friend Day. *Fill me, Lord,* ol' Zeke would pray and cry out to God. Finally a couple of "ecclesiastical observers" got together over the situation. "Why do you suppose Brother Zeke keeps going to the altar and asking the Lord to 'fill' him?" one asked.

"Don't know," the other observer responded. "Guess he leaks!"

Industry, education, and science know how important it is for their professionals to stay on the cutting edge. Thankfully, even the Church understands the importance of a refresher course. Most denominations even give certificates to those who have taken a ministerial refresher course.

Paul found some disciples in Ephesus who needed a refresher course. They needed to be fired up—warmed by the fires of the Holy Spirit.

It's true of New Testament leadership: Every once in a while, the workers need new motivation. Vibrant Christian leaders are not only called to be "instructors," "pastors," and "supervisors"—they're also called to be *motivators*.

Sometimes the ministry candle begins to wane. Sometimes the flame begins to flicker. Sometimes the tired worker needs a glass of lemonade and an encouraging word (and sometimes in that very order). The leader observes the need, rushes to the needy, carefully administers the help and healing, and rejoices over the rejuvenation.

The leader who has discovered the triumphs of teamwork knows the personal cost. Triumphant team ministry includes "honoring one another" by

> finding them
> feeding them
> forming them
> following them and
> firing them

5 MAXIMIZING ENERGY EFFECTIVENESS

THE HUSBAND-AND-WIFE VACATIONERS had paid hundreds of dollars per night to stay at the oceanside getaway in the Caribbean. And one of the activities in the vacation package was a scuba diving session.

Soon they had their scuba gear on and were being taken by motorboat to the dive site. Clear blue waters beckoned them as they turned on their air tanks and leaned backward from the boat into the water.

The quiet beauty at 30 feet was an immediate payoff for the money they had invested. Carrying a waterproof chalkboard, the husband wrote, "This is great!" His wife nodded her approval so excitedly that she almost dislodged her facemask.

Suddenly, to their left they saw another person in the water. He was dressed in casual clothes and didn't have any diving gear. The vacationing divers were amazed as they watched him energetically maneuvering in the water. He would quickly swim upward and then float back toward the ocean bottom. Time and again, he repeated the motions. Intrigued that the man had such maneuverability without diving gear, the husband swam over to the man and wrote on the chalkboard, "Why no gear?"

The man, purplish in complexion, grabbed the chalkboard and wrote frantically: *Boat sank! I'm drowning!*

Almost anyone in Christian ministry understands the man's sinking feeling:

Too much to do.

Too little time.

Not enough help.

Not enough equipment.

Drowning—even in casual clothes!

You don't have any difficulty keeping the Pauline commission "serving the Lord." But you gasp for air when you see the prerequisites: "never lacking in zeal" and "keep your spiritual fervor."

Vibrant Christian leadership isn't just about mission, purpose, vision, and goals. It's also about having enough strength left at the end of the day to be able to face the next one.

The "e" word: "energy." Webster says it comes from the Greek word meaning activity. It's a "vigorous exertion of power."[1] But the more vigorous you are in exerting it, the less powerful you become! And isn't it interesting that the activities recommended to help you gain more energy are the same ones that tire you out?

But energy is vital to Christian ministry in general and Christian leadership more specifically. You may be able to get by with diminishing pay, but you can't continue to function with diminishing energy. Pastor and author Gary Fenton warned:

> Authentic ministry does not depend on our getting a big break; instead, it rests in the awareness of God's call to ministry and the daily offering up of our best efforts. . . . To the young, God gives physical energy and optimism. In mid-life and beyond, He gives wisdom—which helps us know best where to put our energies. But because the church tends to reward the upbeat, go-getting attitudes of youth, a mid-life pastor faces a crisis when he realizes he can no longer "run up the steps," when his energy begins to flag as never before. He may view this change as loss. When this happens, there are usually three temptations: fake it and try to hide any sign of weakness; decide to slow down and coast; quit.[2]

Whether you're on the low end of the age scale or the low end of the energy scale, there's hope from the counsel of God's Word.

"MR. ENERGY"

When you put the words "New Testament leader" and "energy" together, what New Testament character comes to mind? Probably the apostle Peter. He was the disciples' poster boy for attention deficit syndrome! Even when his feet were still, his tongue was usually in motion.

While the other apostles were watching, "the rock" was walking. Nobody topped Peter in zeal. He didn't always do it right, but this much is true: he always did something. One incident underscores the fact. Jesus had just served fish and chips to 5,000 families on a Judean hillside. Amazingly, the apostles were told to leave before the lawn chairs were folded up and the tables put away.

Then, as is often the case in ministry, the apostles' busyness was topped off with a storm!

Immediately Jesus made the disciples get into the boat and go on ahead of him to the other side, while he dismissed the crowd. After he had dismissed them, he went up on a mountainside by himself to pray. When evening came, he was there alone, but the boat was already a considerable distance from land, buffeted by the waves because the wind was against it.

During the fourth watch of the night Jesus went out to them, walking on the lake. When the disciples saw him walking on the lake, they were terrified. "It's a ghost," they said, and cried out in fear.

But Jesus immediately said to them: "Take courage! It is I. Don't be afraid."

"Lord, if it's you," Peter replied, "tell me to come to you on the water."

"Come," he said.

Then Peter got down out of the boat, walked on the water and came toward Jesus. But when he saw the wind, he was afraid and, beginning to sink, cried out, "Lord, save me!"

Immediately Jesus reached out his hand and caught him. "You of little faith," he said, "why did you doubt?"

And when they climbed into the boat, the wind died down. Then those who were in the boat worshiped him, saying, "Truly you are the Son of God" (Matt. 14:22-33).

Peter's oceanic behavior offers us at least three leadership cautions:

1. He started his speech before he did his research.
2. He began the journey before he knew the route.
3. He gave up before he reached his goal.

But at least he tried. The other apostles were locked in a committee meeting, trying to decide who was going to go for the Coast Guard! Oliver Wendell Holmes said, "I find the great thing in this world is not so much where we stand as in what direction we are moving: To reach the port of heaven, we must sail sometimes with the wind and sometimes against it—but we must sail, and not drift, nor lie at anchor."[3] Sometimes, we just need to make a move.

"Take Two Aspirations, and Call Me in the Morning"

At times, *enthusiastic* is even better than *athletic*. A Christian leader who is enthusiastic usually inspires the energy of others. A leader who is athletic inspires only those who are still limber enough to tie their tennis shoes without a standby tank of oxygen.

There's a synergy of enthusiasm. Enthusiastic people are like "energy doctors," indirectly prescribing, "Take two aspirations, and call me in the morning."

The question "What can a leader do to maximize energy effectiveness?" is a worthy one. In answer to this question, let's look at several keys. They may not be conclusive, but we trust they'll be constructive.

Keys to Channeling Energy for Maximum Effectiveness

Key No. 1: Determine what's really important

There's a lot to do in one day. Why, the decisions you have to make even before you get to that first cup of coffee can drain your energy! In fact, just getting dressed can be mind-boggling.

Casual or business?

Skirt or slacks?

Blue suit or brown?

Loafers or wing tips?

High heels or flats?

Printed tie or plain?

Winged collar or straight?

French cuffs or buttons?

Printed pink or frilly plain white?

Sweater or vest?

Argyle socks or plain?

Pleated slacks or straight?

Long sleeves or short?

Golf shirt or button-down?

Aqua Velva or Ralph Lauren?

CVS Pharmacy or Chanel #5?

But the most important decisions in a day are not about appearance—they're about *importance.* Certainly, what you look like is important. But what you *do* is much more important. And what you decide to be—*the most important thing(s)* you do each day—will directly influence your energy flow throughout that day. Willard Peterson said, "Decision is the spark that ignites action. Until a decision is made, nothing happens."

But how do you put purpose into those plans?

A. Is it God-honoring? Will your decided action maintain its integrity once it's strained through the filter of your faith? The standard is clear: "Seek first his kingdom and his righteousness" (Matt. 6:33). Is it a Kingdom priority? If it's not, then it has the potential to drain your energy instead of enhancing it. Elmer Towns said, "Greatness involves more than measurable achievement—it starts with the leader's heart and not his head. It is rooted in virtues like self-sacrifice, love, courage, loyalty, accountability, humility, meaning, mission, passion, and commitment."[4] Those are Kingdom qualities, characteristics of a *Christ-one.* And your decisions must possess His dynamic.

B. Does it have an eternal dimension? Does the proposed action merely result in accumulations on earth, or does it invest in eternity? Actions that are centered in the temporal are energy-drainers. Just ask someone behind the wheel of a "creditmobile"—that flashy, plastic way of life that transports people to the world's paranoia parade—always trying to impress people with something new even before the old is paid for.

Will your proposed action increase your stock in the things of earth, or will it add to your account in Heaven's Savings and Loan?

C. Will it add *quality,* or will it add *quantity?* Those "unclaimed jewels" of Jesus' time, Mary and Martha, struggled with this very issue (Luke 10:38-42). Actually, *both* Mary and Martha of Jesus' day had a problem. Mary was too "heavenly," and Martha was too "earthly." Where's the balance? That's the important question. Once you reach adulthood, chores are usually a choice. But keep adding chores, and the result is fewer *choices!* Chores began to dominate, and soon they siphon your energy reserves.

D. How will it affect my family? The family is a God-given institution, but it doesn't mean we're incarcerated in it. Interpersonal relationships with those we love most should be joyous, not tumultuous. Adding an item to our "to-do list" might not necessarily be good for the family. It's like the elderly man presenting his letter and some pocket change to the postal clerk. The clerk said, "I'm sorry, sir—this letter is too heavy. You're going to have to add another stamp." The man replied sharply, "And I suppose that's going to make it lighter?"

Key No. 2: Train for efficiency

Unlike being a sophomore in college, being in ministry often reminds you that you *don't* know more than you *do* know. Sometimes you just need more training. For example, long-distance runners not only have to learn how to run faster but also must learn how to run "smarter." They need to learn how to pace themselves so that they have enough energy to finish the race. What's the best stride? How do proper rest and nourishment factor in? Does a certain brand of running shoes offer an advantage? The winning begins with the training.

It's the same in ministry:

- Christian leaders need to know how to work smarter.
- Christian leaders need to know how to pace themselves.
- Christian leaders need to learn what "stride" will help them reach their goals.
- Christian leaders need to learn how to factor in nourishment and rest.
- Christian leaders need to know how to equip themselves.

Leith Anderson illustrates the need for updating leadership skills to meet the changes and challenges of new millennium ministry: "Computer skills learned on an AppleIIE do not equip a person to run the latest PC laptop. Graduation from medical school in 1967 may mean that a physician can write 'M.D.' after her name but does not mean that you want her operating on your son. In each of these cases and a million more, it is necessary to be a lifelong learner."[5]

Efficiency aids energy. For example, the mechanically challenged can go through three works of grace, a lifelong relationship, and an entire can of deodorant trying to hook up a dryer. Or that same Bob Villa wannabe can go to the library and check out one of a hundred home improvement videos that could show him or her in a matter of minutes how it's done.

Ministry training resources are everywhere:
> Christian bookstores
> County or college libraries
> Christian Internet sites
> Christian college or university on-line degree programs
> Christian correspondence courses
> Community college or institutional seminars
> Ministerial association events
> Denominational continuing education programs
> Christian college or university summer programs
> High school or college night courses
> Accelerated degree programs
> Retail store symposiums and classes

The excuses for sticking with a Ford technology mind-set in a Ferrari world are beginning to pale. For example, if the majority of workers in your church or organization have computer savvy, you won't make much of an impression bragging about your Royal typewriter (although your Royal may be more dependable!).

Being aware of current ministry methodologies gives the Christian leader a whole new set of options. And the possibility of reducing time and tension restraints will certainly produce greater energy for ministry. However, as E. Glenn Wagner writes, "A person with a sackful of skills but without a tight grip on the promises of God will quickly burn out."[6]

Key No. 3: Focus your efforts

An advertisement on the van of a plumbing business reads, "We've been in the bathroom for 130 years." The company's message is clear: "When it comes to plumbing, we're focused." Focus is important whether you're judging a javelin-throwing contest, supervising the "pin-the tail-on-the-donkey" game at a preschool party, or trying to run a Christian organization.

Christian leaders without focus usually have an energy deficit.

What Fred Smith says about Christian organizations can certainly be said of Christian leaders as well: "No church can accomplish everything. I once heard a pastor say, 'I can't make a mark on infinity. My mark has to be on finiteness.' Maybe huge organizations can accomplish a great array of things, but the average church has to identify its strengths and choose where it will put its efforts."[7]

It's the difference between shooting turkeys with a shotgun and doing so with a bow and arrow. With a shotgun, you aim in the general direction of the turkey and pray that one or more of the pellets will hit its mark. With a bow and arrow, you aim specifically, release the string carefully, and follow the arrow closely. (Then you pray that you didn't accidentally shoot another hunter in the leg!)

Shotgun leadership is energy-depleting. A vibrant Christian leader soon understands that he or she accomplishes little by trying to do *everything!* Remember Jesus' advice to Lazarus's sister during that tension-filled luncheon at Bethany? "'Martha, Martha,' the Lord answered, 'you are worried and upset about many things, but only one thing is needed. Mary has chosen what is better'" (Luke 10:41).

"Better" or "many"? That's the important choice for Christian leaders who want to maximize their effectiveness while they channel their energies.

A. Focus on the Spirit-directed activity. In the classic devotional *A Table in the Wilderness: Daily Meditations from the Ministry of Watchman Nee,* Nee warns:

> Sin before God is of two kinds. One is the sin of refusing to obey when He issues orders; the other is the sin of going ahead when He has issued none. The one is rebellion; not doing what the Lord has commanded. The other is presumption; doing what He has not required. How much of your work for Him has been based on a clear command of the Lord, and how much simply on the ground that it was a good thing to do?

Self-directed leadership instead of Spirit-directed leadership is energy-depleting.

B. Focus on mission-related activity. The story is told of two pilots who had just graduated from flight school (probably by correspondence!). On their approach to the landing strip, with the landing gear inches away from the runway, the copilot suddenly shouted, "Pull up! Pull up!" Frantically, the pilot pulled back on the yoke and circled for another try.

Once again, just as the wheels were about to touch the runway, the copilot shouted, "Pull up! Pull up!" And once again, the pilot pulled up. This scenario continued for three more approaches.

Finally the exasperated copilot remarked, "That's the shortest runway I've seen in all my life!"

The pilot responded, "Yeah, but look how *wide* it is!"

Obviously, the rookie pilots had made their approach from the wrong direction. Flight paths are important in Christian leadership as well. The mission statement of the organization serves to give direction to its activities. When those are ignored, crashes—physical, emotional, financial, or organizational—are inevitable.

Great Nazarene evangelist Uncle Buddy Robinson prayed, "O Lord . . . give me a rhinoceros hide for skin, and hang up a wagon-load of determination in the gable-end of my soul. Help me to sign the contract to fight the devil as long as I've got a tooth." Now that's focus!

Certainly, your mission will be to fight the devil. But it will also have other variations on that theme: evangelism, education, edification, and so on. You can't focus on everything—that's too tiring and too ineffective—but you can focus on the primary mission activities.

C. Focus on people-building activity. Starting at home (1 Tim. 3:12), focus on making people better people. If you've ever been fed up with service at a fast-food restaurant, you know that management isn't spending a lot of people-building time. Most feel fortunate to find a body warm enough to turn off the timer when the french fries are done! Keith Naughton wrote about the industry's lack of people-building activity in a *Newsweek* article. "The luxury of leisurely classroom training for new recruits has all but vanished. Fresh hires at Wal-Mart and McDonald's no longer spend days locked in the back room watching training videos. Most training comes on the job, and if the rookie needs more, he can log on to the computer in the break room." He quotes one recruiter: "We used to teach them the history of the potato, but they don't need all that to make fries."[8]

People-building takes time and energy. But the results are eventually time- and energy-conserving. That's because people who have been given good skills, information, and motivation duplicate the achievements of the trainer many times over. The Timothy principle works: "The things you have heard me say in the presence of many witnesses entrust to reliable men who will also be qualified to teach others" (2 Tim. 2:2).

Key No. 4: Conserve your strength

If some Christian workers conserved any more strength, they

would have to wear a belt with one of those "backing up" warning beepers clipped to it! But generally, Christian workers are moving forward, running on so little gas they would short-circuit a "low fuel" light on an auto dashboard.

You've been there. You're tired of being tired. You're on your sixth day of strength, and "Sunday's coming!" It's a dangerous predicament.

- You're spiritually vulnerable.
- You begin to overlook key details.
- Your relationships are strained.
- Your corporate work replaces your personal worship.
- Your efforts are less effective.

Former Wheaton College president Hudson T. Armerding wrote of those who fell victim to their own vulnerability: "Part of the reason for their error in judgment is their tendency to quantify their work, whereas God's criterion is quality."[9]

Doing more (and often for less) seems to be the mark of new millennium ministry. And as a result, effectiveness has taken it on the chin! But we can maintain solid oak effectiveness in a forest of weeping willow activity! Let's try to reduce it to the simplest formula. We suggest a "3-D" approach to conserving energy and maximizing effectiveness: *designate, delegate,* and *disassociate.*

A. Designate. Every leader needs to assign a priority level to his or her work. Almost every business management system recommends it—but too often it is ignored. We have already discussed important and focused efforts. But how do you put tags on them? Whether you use A-B-C files, marked file drawers, PDA programs, or PC organizational charts, somehow you must avoid lumping all work together on the same desktop! Designate it:

Priority One work needs immediate attention. It's the letter that needs an immediate answer, the proposal that needs an immediate writing, the telephone or personal call that needs immediate handling. It's work that will jeopardize your personal or managerial credibility if it's not taken care of in a timely fashion.

Priority Two work needs attention in the near future. It's that manuscript that a friend asked you to read when you have the time. It's the birthday or anniversary gift that needs to be purchased for the celebration that will be held two to three weeks from now. It's anything that deserves focused time and effort within a given time frame in order to facilitate a person or program.

Priority Three work doesn't need immediate attention. It's that book or novel someone recommended and then parked in your "in" box. It's that group picture of your grade school outing to the zoo that you want to eventually frame. It's anything that could be done now, but could also be done during an indefinite period of time.

New Testament leader and writer John seemed to receive a progressive/priority plan when he was given the Revelation: "Write, therefore, what you have seen, what is now and what will take place later" (Rev. 1:19). Alone on the isle of Patmos without an administrative assistant, a Palm Pilot, or pastoral staff, he probably couldn't have handled the whole panorama of time's events at once—any more than we can handle the whole scope of ministry at once.

It's like the proverbial instruction to the pizza maker: "Cut my pizza into four pieces—I couldn't possibly eat twelve." Life just seems a little easier in smaller chunks.

B. Delegate. Determine which of the tasks over which you have claimed ownership could be shared with another. Smith and Lindsay speak of leadership in terms of becoming "an agent of change": "When you move from personal mastery to becoming an agent of change on behalf of others, you move into the sphere of interpersonal and organizational influence. Before you identify people, issues, or programs that you believe need to be changed, you must understand that since others are part of the issues, they must be part of the strategic planning for transformation."[10] The choice is clear: *involve or dissolve!*

Some leaders can't change a lightbulb. Others seem to be able to move organizational mountains with a tongue depressor. What's the difference? Creative ownership. Until principles or actions have become the property of the group instead of the private stash of the leader, nothing will happen!

Using Eccles. 4:9 (NLT) as a theme ("Two people can accomplish more than twice as much as one"), the Christian Business Men's Committee of USA proposed six *e-n-e-r-g-y* creating principles in their faxed newsletter, "The Fax of Life." They are helpful in considering how to create energy through teamwork.

E mphasize the best in each other.

N ever try to control each other.

E ncourage the free flow of ideas.

R eplace competition with cooperation.

G ive away what you have . . . and watch it multiply!

Y ield the credit to others. Remember: you're a team!

If every Christian has a spiritual gift—and every Christian does —then the job of the Christian leader is to act like a two-year-old on Christmas Day: vigorously unwrapping everyone else's gifts!

Leader, you were meant to *mentor*. Jesus' chain-link principle of leadership hasn't been changed: "As you sent me into the world, I have sent them into the world" (John 17:18). The evangelizing of the world is dependent upon saved people seeking, certifying, and sending others—over and over again, until the Lord Jesus Christ opens the curtains of heaven.

And it's happening!

Church growth leader and pulse-taker Thom S. Rainer said:

> Our research has shown a trend of increased interest in mentoring over the past six years. Some Christian leaders mentor those who are specifically called by God to vocational ministry. Others focus their mentoring efforts on laypersons, to better equip them for their work in the local church. We would not be surprised to discover a few years from now that even more leaders view mentoring as one of their leadership strengths.[11]

Got energy? Delegate.

C. Disassociate. Let it go! Often, handing work off to another leader or a developing leader is harder than selling golf clubs to a boa constrictor: the principle is there, but the potential is restrictive! Even more difficult is making the assignment and then letting go.

It's like the teen who finally got a job as the head cook at the Dairy Queen. One day he made a call to the store's manager. Putting a handkerchief over the phone's mouthpiece to disguise his voice, the young worker said, "I'm calling about the head cook position."

"We already have a cook," the manager responded.

"Is that right? Well, may I ask how he is doing?"

"Fine," the manager answered. "Just fine!"

"Boy, am I glad to hear that!" the caller exclaimed.

"Who is this?" the slightly agitated manager asked.

The teen answered with relief, "I'm the head cook, and I just wanted to check on myself!"

You've heard the expression "Relax—you got the job!" In other words, the assignment has been signed, sealed, and delivered. It's too late to fret.

We could also say, "Relax—you *assigned* the job!" Once the work designation is made, and once the work delegation has been assigned, the surefire way to burn unnecessary energy is to let it dominate your thinking. Paul made the wonderful discovery of letting go. "I know whom I have believed, and am persuaded that he is able to keep that which I have committed unto him against that day" (2 Tim. 1:12, KJV).

It's a principle as simple as the age-old adage "Don't cry over spilled milk." Some things simply aren't worth the effort:

- Trying to stop that ring in the water after tossing in the pebble.
- Getting out of the car to check your tire pressure in an automatic car wash.
- Trying to keep Grandma from seeing the sale rack in the children's section of a discount store.
- Trying to convince a telemarketer that "no" means "no."
- Asking the regular attendees of the church to sit in one of the front pews.

Worrying over your previous actions is a time-waster—and an energy-exhauster. Let it go! The Master didn't pull any punches at this point. "Who of you by worrying can add a single hour to his life?" (Matt. 6:27).

Key No. 5: Strengthen your faith

Another great energy-drainer is a softening faith. "Never be lacking in zeal, but keep your spiritual fervor, serving the Lord" (Rom. 12:11). King David understood what happens when the soul gets out of sorts with the Sovereign Lord:

> Surely you desire truth in the inner parts; you teach me wisdom in the inmost place. Cleanse me with hyssop, and I will be clean; wash me, and I will be whiter than snow. Let me hear joy and gladness; let the bones you have crushed rejoice. Hide your face from my sins and blot out all my iniquity. Create in me a

pure heart, O God, and renew a steadfast spirit within me *(Ps. 51:6-10)*.

Things looked pretty good on the outside—the kingdom was running smoothly, the praise team had rehearsed and was in place, and WD-40 had been sprayed on the managerial machinery. But in the basement of David's heart, the light of God's presence was on its last watt. "Surely you desire truth in the inner parts." That spiritual dimness affected his physical and spiritual energy. Notice the effects, and notice David's prayer for renewal:

1. A sense of uncleanness—"cleanse me . . . and I will be clean."
2. A sense of unhappiness—"let me hear joy."
3. A sense of unwholesomeness—"let the bones you have crushed rejoice."
4. A sense of unworthiness—"blot out all my iniquity."
5. A sense of unsteadiness—"renew a steadfast spirit within me."

Personal revival may be one of the greatest needs in Christian leadership today. The psalmist didn't say, "Revive *them.*" He said, "Revive *us*" (Ps. 85:6, emphasis added). He didn't intimate that the heathen were in need of a fresh spiritual touch. He suggested that the needy ones were the righteous ones—those who are already well-known in heaven.

Look a little bit farther back in the Book, and you'll see that the hands of God's leaders sag at times. In fact, Moses' whole body tired as he captained the battle against the Amalekites. The remedy is beautiful. God moved in. Not only did the Creator form a chair for the chairman of the board, but He also even provided a committee of arm-lifters to stand alongside. "When Moses' hands grew tired, they took a stone and put it under him and he sat on it. Aaron and Hur held his hands up—one on one side, one on the other—so that his hands remained steady till sunset" (Exod. 17:12).

Educator and author David J. Spittal wrote, "It is easy to be mesmerized by personalities and mega-leaders within the church. Both God-ordained leaders and followers should remember that the church does not thrive because of these leaders, or us. The church thrives because it is only through the body and blood of Jesus Christ mediated through His Spirit that it receives sustenance, purpose and power."[12]

There it is. Ultimately, vibrant Christian leadership is not about skills. It's about source.

Too much work, with too little energy, and pretty soon *spiritual dryness* begins to hinder the flow of God's promises and power into our lives.

The New Testament writer put it on parchment:

No discipline seems pleasant at the time, but painful. Later on, however, it produces a harvest of righteousness and peace for those who have been trained by it. Therefore, strengthen your feeble arms and weak knees. "Make level paths for your feet," so that the lame may not be disabled, but rather healed. Make every effort to live in peace with all men and to be holy; without holiness no one will see the Lord. See to it that no one misses the grace of God and that no bitter root grows up to cause trouble and defile many *(Heb. 12:11-15)*.

Sometimes we take up residence in a subleased pit. But the ol' cowpoke philosopher once again points out, "If you find yourself in a hole, the first thing to do is stop digging." There are some things we can do besides adding a widescreen television set to the place: we can work toward strengthening our faith.

First, surrender your struggle over your circumstances. Toil and tears are part of the harvest process. "No discipline seems pleasant at the time, but painful. Later on, however, it produces a harvest of righteousness and peace" (v. 11). The soil is painfully broken up during the planting. The seeds are sown by the bone-weary efforts of the sower. The sun often burns the harvester. Established things are rearranged. There is cutting. Production is not a comfortable process—but the results are wholeness and fruit.

Struggling with the "process" is a waste of energy.

In *Secrets of the Vine,* Bruce Wilkinson describes the care of the vinedresser who spots a sagging vine, cleans it, and then lifts it up from its proximity to the ground so that its new height will make it more fruitful: "After all, the Vinedresser has only abundance and joy—not misery—in mind when He tends to a dirty branch. As soon as the branch is cleaned up and ready to thrive, the need for interventions ends."[13]

Second, acknowledge your weakness. "Strengthen your feeble arms and weak knees" (v. 12). The boxing coach watches the match closely.

He looks for some telltale signs that his boxer is weakening: the gloves aren't being held as high; there's unsteadiness; when the blows come, the knees buckle; there's backward movement instead of forward. He knows that the tide of the fight is turning toward the foe. Soon the bell will ring. The boxer will return to his corner and in the next hurried moments, the handlers will do everything possible to rejuvenate the competitor. Water. Salve. Spirits. Words of encouragement. Words of instruction. All these go into immediate motion.

On one occasion, Paul went to his corner bruised and battered from a three-round fight. And heaven's handlers were there. But before he got help, he had to admit he needed it:

> To keep me from becoming conceited because of these surpassingly great revelations, there was given me a thorn in my flesh, a messenger of Satan, to torment me. Three times I pleaded with the Lord to take it away from me. But he said to me, "My grace is sufficient for you, for my power is made perfect in weakness." Therefore I will boast all the more gladly about my weaknesses, so that Christ's power may rest on me. That is why, for Christ's sake, I delight in weaknesses, in insults, in hardships, in persecutions, in difficulties. For when I am weak, then I am strong (2 Cor. 12:7-10).

The greatest strength is available even in the weakest times. For example, electrical power is available to all the rooms of your home. But when an overload occurs, part of the system shuts down. For your protection, a circuit breaker in your house's electrical panel usually shuts that section down. If the homeowner wants power to be restored, he or she doesn't go into denial. No, it's a trip to the electrical panel to look for the circuit breaker that's off, search for areas of overload in the house, reduce the overload, and then go back to flip the switch. Power is restored.

The discerning (and experienced) homeowner can usually tell by the flickering lights or momentary power interruptions that the system is beginning to overload. Ignoring those signs will result in total loss of power. But acknowledging them is the first step toward renewed power.

Third, understand that your spiritual strength influences others. "'Make level paths for your feet,' so that the lame may not be disabled, but rather healed" (Heb. 12:13). If the leader starts taking shortcuts, others will not only follow but may get lost! One of life's great time-wasters is to get into a car with a driver who thinks there's an easier way to get somewhere—especially if he or she ignores the directions of experienced travelers. From the moment you close the passenger-side door, you're in danger of jeopardizing your arrival time (and often your friendship).

The wisdom writer warned, "There is a way that seems right to a man, but in the end it leads to death" (Prov. 14:12). Not every road leads home. And not every bypass will save you time—especially when it comes to matters of the heart. Remember: some people whom you love are following your route with great curiosity.

Fourth, determine to make purity of heart the mark of your success. "Make every effort to live in peace with all men and to be holy; without holiness no one will see the Lord" (Heb. 12:14). Of course, that verse can be dissected, discoursed, diagrammed, and delivered in more ways than Wonder enriches bread! But you can't get away from the fact that people "see the Lord" through the life of their leader.

A strengthened faith makes altar vows—not just a wedding altar, ordination altar, or Communion altar, but the altar of the heart, the place of "living sacrifices" (Rom. 12:1), where New Testament leaders burned their declarations of independence in the fires of Pentecost.

Ultimately, it makes no difference how powerful, prominent, purposeful, or personable you are if you don't have a pure heart. Seek that first. Seek that forever.

Fifth, dig up the roots of bitterness. "See to it that no one misses the grace of God and that no bitter root grows up to cause trouble and defile many" (Heb. 12:15). Weeds hide healthy blades of grass. And weeds are not something you put on the list of amenities for your home tour.

That cowpoke philosopher said, "It don't take a genius to spot a goat in a flock of sheep." Being around someone who's growing a root of bitterness is about as unpleasant as being in a clothes closet with a porcupine that has whooping cough!

You just can't keep bitterness to yourself. It not only infects you but also spreads to everyone you come in contact with. It "grows up" to "defile many." It must be dealt with quickly and humbly. If it isn't, it will sap your emotional, physical, and spiritual energy.

The need of the hour is great: "Never lacking in zeal, but keep your spiritual fervor, serving the Lord" (Rom. 12:11). But when you add the word "Lord," you've added the very supply sufficient for every act of personal devotion or corporate leadership.

⑥ ADJUSTING TO ADVERSITY

THE ADVICE CAME IN ONE OF THOSE E-mail messages that appear like the Ghost of Christmas Past on your computer during the night. Though you may know who delivered them on the doorsteps of your Internet portal, you never really know where they originate. But sometimes they say in print what you've been muttering in your spirit.

This one was on managing stress. It told its readers to visualize themselves in a picturesque garden setting—a solitary place, far away from the phone, fax machine, or fatty acids of time.

"The soothing sound of a gentle waterfall fills the air with a cascade of serenity. The water is clear. You can easily make out the face of the person whose head you're holding under the water." It closes, "There now—feeling better?"

Now, we know that none of our readers ever feel like participating in "extreme baptisms"! But now and then Christian leaders meet people and problems that send them packing the Samsonite in their minds for a sudden getaway (especially when you're on staff and the company car is a U-Haul truck).

Harlan Cleveland said, "Leaders are problem-solvers by talent and temperament, and by choice. For them, the new information environment—undermining old means of control, opening up old closets of secrecy, reducing the relevance of ownership, early arrival, and location—should seem less a litany of problems than an agenda for action."[1] In other words, when the going gets tough, the tough learn how to tough it out!

It's not uncommon. In Christian leadership, one minute you're the guest of honor at the head table, and the next minute you're the table covering, sitting used and crumpled near the side door of the fellowship hall. In between are the misunderstandings, missteps, and miscommunications of Christian leadership "under construction." Cleveland calls those challenges "an agenda for action."

You should get a merit badge for learning to deal with adversity. But you probably won't. You'll just get another matching set of circumstances that will call for more attention than you can give, more wisdom than you can muster, and more patience than you can squeeze out of that "last nerve."

There's no way that one chapter—or one book—can teach you how to handle the people or problems facing *your* organization. But here are a few heartfelt suggestions that we pray will be of some help to you as the leader.

1. Look for the advantage in the adversity

The Christian leader is a negotiator. He or she learns to walk the fine line between being obstinate over ideals and being merciful over methods. Argus Hamilton, former columnist for *The Oklahoman* newspaper, once told the story of a Tibetan monk who allegedly lived to be 120 years old. Asked on his 120th birthday how he achieved such a milestone, the monk replied, "When I was 83 I decided not to argue with anyone."

The reporter challenged the monk: "I can't believe that. There must be some other reasons you lived to this age. You probably ate the right things. You must have gotten eight hours of sleep at night. You probably learned how to meditate on good thoughts or something."

The old monk stared at the reporter a few seconds and then replied quietly, "Maybe you're right."

Some settlements aren't as easily reached. New Testament leader Silas learned that firsthand.

Silas was on Paul's team. (That should have been his first clue to keep the canvas coverings off the lifeboats.) Paul's travel plans always included the unexpected port of call.

> Five times I received from the Jews the forty lashes minus one. Three times I was beaten with rods, once I was stoned, three times I was shipwrecked, I spent a night and a day in the open sea, I have been constantly on the move. I have been in danger from rivers, in danger from bandits, in danger from my own countrymen, in danger from Gentiles; in danger in the city, in danger in the country, in danger at sea; and in danger from false brothers. I have labored and toiled and have often gone without sleep; I have known hunger and thirst and have often

gone without food; I have been cold and naked. Besides every-thing else, I face daily the pressure of my concern for all the churches (*2 Cor. 11:24-28*).

Interesting words—"Besides everything else, I face daily the pressures of my concern for all the churches." Eugene Peterson has an interesting interpretation of that phrase in *The Message:* "And that's not the half of it, when you throw in the daily pressures and anxieties of all the churches." In addition to the attacks from with-out, there are some in-house dangers:

What's worse than a beating? A business meeting that's gone awry.

What's worse than a shipwreck? Staff failures.

What's worse than dangers in the land, sea, or air? Division in the church or organization.

Come to think of it, some Christian organizations are like mili-tary boot camps, where the troops strengthen their muscles with too little sleep, too little nourishment, and too little kindness. But it's there—in the struggle for survival—that future leaders are first melted and then molded.

Silas and Paul survived the predicament with a praise chorus on their lips. Acts 16:23-25 says,

> After they had been severely flogged, they were thrown into prison, and the jailer was commanded to guard them carefully. Upon receiving such orders, he put them in the inner cell and fastened their feet in the stocks. About midnight Paul and Silas were praying and singing hymns to God, and the other prisoners were listening to them.

Silas was a charter member of Jerusalem First Church (the downtown one). Bible scholars suggest that he was probably a Hel-lenistic Jew and a Roman citizen. Other than that, little is known of this New Testament leader. We do know that he humbly learned to tame adversity by turning it into *advantage*. The politicians threw him into jail to prevent him from witnessing. But notice: "the other prisoners were listening." Silas didn't change his message; rather, he simply changed pulpits—along with his attitude. The winds of ad-versity filled his lungs with praise!

There are several ways we can learn how to make an advantage out of an adversity.

A. Learn to jibe when the winds change. "Jibe" is a sailing term. The dictionary defines it: "To change a vessel's course when sailing with the wind so that as the stern passes through the eye of the wind the boom swings to the opposite side."[2] Any weekend sailor knows the feeling of having the sails adjusted properly, moving smoothly across the choppy waters with a "good wind," and then needing to make a sudden left turn to catch the changing wind direction.

The turn begins the turmoil!

Wind quickly (and often violently) fills the sails, sending the boom in flight.

The sailor learns in a hurry that when it comes to being on the water, "duck" isn't just a referral to that cute little bird floating daintily on top. "Coming about!" the sailor shouts to the passengers. That's nautical talk for "Duck! You're about to get hit in the head!"

Used properly, the "jibe" is done with little or no pain, the turn is made, the sails are readjusted, and the vessel is on its victorious way again. It uses the wind change as a power, not a problem.

Have you ever been caught in the winds of a sudden "jibe"? You changed the time of a service, and one would think you changed the order of the universe! In a *Leadership* article titled "Making Changes Without Getting People Steamed," Larry W. Osborne quotes an old farmer: "Go slow. Churches are a lot like horses. They don't like to be startled or surprised. It causes deviant behavior." And he adds, "The fiercest battles are seldom fought over theology. More often, they are fought over change, sometimes even the slightest change." Osborne suggests some steps for making changes (making a jibe when the winds change):

- Test the waters—find out how people will react should the change take place.
- Listen and respond to resisters—rather than view them as enemies to be overcome . . . see them as advisers.
- Talk to individuals before groups—share with enough individuals to give an idea credibility.
- Lead boldly—stepping forward to champion a cause: clearly making . . . views known and doing everything . . . to persuade the holdouts to follow.[3]

The good news is that the winds of adversity often cause a positive updraft:

People start communicating.

Ideas are batted about.

Solutions begin to sink or surface.

Leadership is identified.

Hidden agendas are posted.

The vibrant Christian leader learns to make good use of the "jibes." He or she uses the strengths of the adversity to an advantage. Course corrections are made (with proper warning: "Duck!"), and the ship sails on.

Leadership mentor Dick Wynn quotes Jessica Tandy, Oscar winner for her role in the film *Driving Miss Daisy*, who was asked if any of her performances had left her unsatisfied. She replied, "All of them. I have never come off the stage at the end of a performance and said, 'Tonight, everything was perfect.' There will always be some little thing that I'll have to get right tomorrow."[4]

Course corrections arising out of adversity can be a positive thing. Joseph D. Allison gave Christian leaders a workable plan for making positive changes and leading people through times of trouble, times when things are turned upside down:

D   Diagnosis. List factors that caused the problem. What circumstances allowed the error to produce the final result?

C   Contingency. Make plans for dealing with similar problems. Learn to identify those problems earlier in the process.

B   Budget. Allow extra time, extra energy, and extra money for every project.

A   Accountability. Enlist someone on the team to check your progress in making changes.[5]

On September 11, 2001, the sudden and horrible winds of adversity changed the course of almost everyone's journey. New York City's World Trade Center, filled with people from over 80 countries, was attacked and destroyed, resulting in considerable loss of life. Moments later, Washington, D.C.'s Pentagon was bombarded as well, destroying a portion of the building and killing many. Rescuers had to be mobilized. Hearts needed encouragement. Hope needed to be raised like a banner over the burning rubble of a nation blindsided by an explosion of uncontrollable anger. Churches and their leaders rushed to help, using the very adversity to preach the advantages of faith.

Adversity brought sudden attention to the core mission. Churches were soon filled with seeking hearts, where pastors and teachers had the message already in place. Instead of succumbing to the events, Christian workers rose to the occasion, giving cups of cold water, counseling the grief-stricken and fearful, turning their energies to rebuilding shattered lives, sharing resources with those who had suffered setbacks.

Adversity is a wake-up call to the Church.

Adversity is also a notice that life is subject to change without notice.

B. Don't be afraid to change the order of service. On the Sunday following the attack on the United States, it wasn't business as usual in Church. The order of service had suddenly changed. Any pastor or worship leader who ignored the change was seen as unpatriotic at best and insensitive at worst.

There are times when the order of service needs to be abandoned, when the master plan needs either a master overhaul or a master abandonment. And sometimes the abandonment becomes an advantage. The same cowpoke philosopher who advised, "Never squat with yer spurs on," also said, "Never miss a good chance to shut up." Sometimes the greatest victories are won with the noblest surrender.

Charlie Lubin succeeded after such a surrender. Charlie made cheesecake. In fact, his cheesecake was so good that he decided to open a store on the north side of Chicago and make his cheesecake available to the public. People bought it. They bought so much that he opened another store on the south side of the city. But people didn't buy as much cheesecake at the south store. Soon Charlie decided the time wasn't right for cheesecake selling, so he closed both stores.

Later, sitting at the kitchen table, eating his own cheesecake, he decided, "This really *is* good cheesecake. I'm going to open those stores again!" He did—with the same results.

Three more times Charlie started the cheesecake business. And three more times he made the decision to close his stores.

Several months later, Charlie sat at the same kitchen table—eating the same Charlie Lubin-quality cheesecake. And he came to the same conclusion: "This really *is* good cheesecake."

Charlie opened another cheesecake store. But this time he changed the name on the packaging of his cheesecake. He named it after his daughter: Sara Lee.

And people have been buying Charlie's cheesecakes ever since!

If the tides have irreversibly turned, then maybe it's time to stop and rename your organizational cheesecake. In other words, move on to another item on the agenda.

Some staunch positions are ultimately not worth the effort. In the golden glow of eternity, the shades of pink or blue on the wall of that new church nursery won't matter. Beyond the heavenly gates, whether or not someone failed to memorize the organization's employee handbook won't be of greatest consequence. The greatest consequence will be his or her arrival in heaven.

Souls are more important than sales.

Ideals are more important than ideas.

Ministry is more important than management.

The ultimate act of Christian leadership is redemption. Whatever it costs (without compromising Spirit-directed mission or purpose) to influence an "alien" to become a "fellow citizen" and "member of God's household" (see Eph. 2:19) is worth the price—even if that price means altering or abandoning a plan or program.

C. Use prayer as a change agent. Elijah the prophet knew the power of prayer to change hearts. Four hundred fifty prophets of Baal were simply no match for one prayer warrior. It was an awesome scene. The Baal worshipers begged and cried to their god to bring the plans of the prophet to a standstill. And then Elijah prayed: "O LORD, God of Abraham, Isaac and Israel, let it be known today that you are God in Israel and that I am your servant and have done all these things at your command. Answer me, O LORD, answer me, so these people will know that you, O LORD, are God, and that you are turning their hearts back again" (1 Kings 18:36-37)

And what a thousand flyers and paid television ads couldn't do to change society, God did in answer to prayer. "Then the fire of the LORD fell and burned up the sacrifice, the wood, the stones and the soil, and also licked up the water in the trench. When all the people saw this, they fell prostrate and cried, 'The LORD—he is God! The LORD—he is God!'" (vv. 38-39).

The Early Church met under a cloud of uncertainty. The disciples, Peter and John, had prayed over a crippled man lying near the Temple instead of giving him a donation. He was healed, and the political and religious leaders were outraged. They knew they couldn't excommunicate the servants of Christ. They got nervous when the people started praising the Lord in the midst of the problem, so they simply let the disciples go.

The Church met together to discuss the situation among themselves and ended up talking to God. (Good move!)

> After they prayed, the place where they were meeting was shaken. And they were all filled with the Holy Spirit and spoke the word of God boldly (*Acts 4:31*).

Several important principles rise to the surface in the events of Acts 4:

1. *Positive prayers are more effective than pitiful pleadings.* "After further threats they let them go. They could not decide how to punish them, because all the people were praising God for what had happened" (v. 21). The "court" was baffled by the praises of the people over the healing of the crippled man. The same court would have bristled had the Church taken a contentious stand and vehemently argued their case or had begun a "whining campaign."

2. *Evidence is the best defense.* "The man who was miraculously healed was over forty years old" (v. 22). This was an instant deliverance for a long-term condition—evidence of the mighty power of God working in the lives of the disciples. Paul said to New Testament leader Titus, "In everything set them an example by doing what is good. In your teaching show integrity, seriousness and soundness of speech that cannot be condemned, so that those who oppose you may be ashamed because they have nothing bad to say about us" (Titus 2:7-8).

3. *Prayer circles are more potent than public forums.* "Peter and John went back to their own people and reported all that the chief priests and elders had said to them" (v. 23). Jesus suggested that the prayer circle doesn't have to be very large to make big changes: "If two of you on earth agree about anything you ask for, it will be done for you by my Father in heaven. For where two or three come together in my name, there am I with them" (Matt. 18:19-20). Airing dirty laundry fouls the air. Bringing complicated concerns to a concentrated group that understands "Prayer changes things" is a powerful tool for changing things.

4. *Prayer changes the pray-ers.* "After they prayed, the place where they were meeting was shaken. And they were all filled with

the Holy Spirit and spoke the word of God boldly" (v. 31). Prayer is a change agent that alters not only the surroundings ("the place") but also the individual spirit—as well as the corporate ministry.

Recuperating from a back ailment, Ben Patterson, Hope College's dean of chapel, asked for the church directory. Feeling both helpless and bored, he attempted to make what contribution he could to his local congregation. He began to pray through the directory, bringing the needs of his congregation before the Lord one at a time. Soon the "work" of praying became very meaningful. Toward the end of his convalescence, he lamented the fact that he would no longer have the three to four hours a day to pray. Patterson said the Lord seemed to rebuke him and reminded him that the hours in the day were still 24 in number. He would still have time to pray.

He writes,

> I began to understand that God loves the little things, the secret things His servants do, because when we stop being lords, He can be Lord of His church. And when He is Lord, there is power, and there is fruit. The good fruit visible in the church is planted in prayers prayed in weakness and in secret. What happens in prayer is to the spiritual realm what the first two weeks of life are to the physical.[6]

There's something else to consider when adjusting to adversity. The adjustment not only benefits the organization but is a source of enrichment as well.

2. Grow through the crisis

Jeren Rowell wrote about a rookie umpire who stood behind the plate at his first game. Legendary fastball pitcher Nolan Ryan was on the mound. The second pitch of the game was so fast that the umpire didn't know where it was until he heard the "POP!" of the catcher's mitt. He froze. Finally he uttered a faint call: "Strike."

The batter stepped out of the box, went over to the umpire, and patted him on the shoulder. "Don't feel bad, sir. I didn't see it either."

Rowell adds, "Sometimes I feel like that rookie umpire when I try to keep up with the changes happening in our world. Things are changing at fastball speed."[7]

Things are changing quickly and drastically in our world. But adversity is the staging area for personal growth. It's the place where leaders learn to focus on the things that are eternal, not temporal or fleeting. Again, that's seen in the New Testament Church. When religious fanatics martyred the apostle Stephen, the Church experienced great fallout.

> On that day a great persecution broke out against the church at Jerusalem, and all except the apostles were scattered throughout Judea and Samaria. Godly men buried Stephen and mourned deeply for him. But Saul began to destroy the church. Going from house to house, he dragged off men and women and put them in prison.
>
> Those who had been scattered preached the word wherever they went. Philip went down to a city in Samaria and proclaimed the Christ there. When the crowds heard Philip and saw the miraculous signs he did, they all paid close attention to what he said (*Acts 8:1-6*).

The Church's reaction to the adversity is a valuable lesson to 21st-century Christians and Christian organizations struggling with political and religious uncertainties.

A. There was a natural and important grieving process. "Godly men buried Stephen and mourned deeply for him." When the walls came tumbling down, it was of no practical use for the Church to go to the corner discount drugstore and buy a new pair of rose-colored glasses. The security of its leadership had been drastically threatened.

The wisdom writer said, "[There is] a time to kill and a time to heal, a time to tear down and a time to build, a time to weep and a time to laugh, a time to mourn and a time to dance" (Eccles. 3:3-4).

Mourning has its place. The human heart has a reservoir of tears that's factory-installed. Ignoring pain doesn't eliminate it. The function of pain when it comes to a broken or sprained ankle is the classic example. The pain is the signal to put activity on "pause" for the sake of the healing.

Reflection—and even remorse—is part of the healing process. Growth comes by recognizing the end of one episode and the beginning of another. Paul advised that "straining toward what is ahead" begins with "forgetting what is behind" (Phil. 3:13). But just as he "learned to be content" (4:11), "forgetting" was also a process. It takes time to sort through the effects of sudden and hurtful adversity.

But there's no place for hopeless mourning. From the strengths of his New Testament leadership, Paul advised the Church, fearful over its losses and the unknown end times,

> Brothers, we do not want you to be ignorant about those who fall asleep, or to grieve like the rest of men, who have no hope. We believe that Jesus died and rose again and so we believe that God will bring with Jesus those who have fallen asleep in him. According to the Lord's own word, we tell you that we who are still alive, who are left till the coming of the Lord, will certainly not precede those who have fallen asleep. For the Lord himself will come down from heaven, with a loud command, with the voice of the archangel and with the trumpet call of God, and the dead in Christ will rise first. After that, we who are still alive and are left will be caught up together with them in the clouds to meet the Lord in the air. And so we will be with the Lord forever. Therefore encourage each other with these words *(1 Thess. 4:13-18)*.

The Church was encouraged to remember that the final verdict won't come by the words and deeds of its enemies. It will come from its dearest Friend. The last word will come from the one who spoke the first! The Lord himself will have the final say. As the psalmist reminded, weeping is for the night, but joy comes in the morning. In other words, weeping has its place, but it is a temporary reaction compared to the eternal satisfaction.

B. There was a multiplication of troubles before there was a subtraction. It's like the old saying "Somebody told me, 'Cheer up—things could be worse.' So I cheered up, and sure enough—things got worse!" Jesus cautioned His followers about thinking that the battles of time won't have any casualties: "In this world you will have trouble. But take heart! I have overcome the world" (John 16:33).

Every experienced Christian leader understands that church problems are like dominoes set upright in a row. When the first one falls, the others are influenced, one by one, until the last one has tumbled. Jesus talked about the tribulations of the Church in the end times as being "the beginning of sorrows" (Matt. 24:8, KJV). But even in the *multiplication of trouble* He offered the hope of its *final subtraction:* "But take heart! I have overcome the world."

C. There was a harvest amid the horror. "Those who had been scattered preached the word wherever they went" (Acts 8:4). From the catacombs of Rome to the catastrophes of modern times, the Church's finest hour often comes when things are at their worst. Times of adversity are times when, as John Maxwell said, the Church needs to "get the seed out of the barn." The soil has been cultivated by confusion. It's a good time to sow the seeds of hope and forgiveness.

Experience shows that in every calamity, whether a national tragedy or a local church disruption, there's a person who needs to be comforted. Times of confusion reveal the doubtful or the down-trodden—one at a time. These become the Christian leader's hour of opportunity. A word of hope. The plan of salvation. Contributions. Counsel. The times that try our souls are the times when our souls are tender to truth.

D. There was a revelation of God's power. "When the crowds heard Philip and saw the miraculous signs he did, they all paid close attention to what he said" (Acts 8:6). Some of the greatest spiritual miracles are birthed during the greatest earthly adversities. Needs are miraculously supplied. Hearts are miraculously tendered. Enemies are miraculously reconciled. Leadership miraculously surfaces. Jesus is still the master of the raging seas!

The Church learned that lesson in a prison letter from the apostle Paul:

> Now I want you to know, brothers, that what has happened to me has really served to advance the gospel. As a result, it has become clear throughout the whole palace guard and to everyone else that I am in chains for Christ. Because of my chains, most of the brothers in the Lord have been encouraged to speak the word of God more courageously and fearlessly (Phil. 1:12-14).

His courage and fearlessness was released while he was in chains! That sounds as natural as a trained cat, but it's true. The very adversity that Paul's enemies had intended to use to stamp out the gospel actually helped to spread it.

Remember that God created order out of chaos in the first place (Gen. 1). God has the power to transform a mess into a miracle!

3. Live above the level of adversity

Adversity often seeks to be your master. It even tries to control where you live. You seek a temple of worship in the high mountains of faith—it wants you to pitch a pup tent in the valley of despair. Actually, your residence is a personal decision and one that will affect your personal influence or that of your organization.

Paul taught the importance of focus to the New Testament church.

> Since, then, you have been raised with Christ, set your hearts on things above, where Christ is seated at the right hand of God. Set your minds on things above, not on earthly things. For you died, and your life is now hidden with Christ in God. When Christ, who is your life, appears, then you also will appear with him in glory *(Col. 3:1-4).*

Truly, it's a matter of focus. Focus on the adversity, and there will be adverse consequences. Focus on faith, and there will be a positive outcome. Several key actions are highlighted in the apostle's advice.

A. Focus on your position. "You have been raised with Christ" (Col. 3:1). You may not be an appointed bishop. You may be the assistant to the substitute teacher in junior church (and you've been struggling for months to get your turn at using the "chair and whip" on some Sunday morning—but the substitute never gets sick!). But even there—second fiddle to a second fiddle—your position in Christ puts you on a spiritual level above the approximately 4 billion people of the earth who do not claim Him as their Savior.

God is your Father.

Jesus is your Brother.

And the Holy Spirit is not only your constant Companion and Guide but also your blood-signed guarantee of a mansion over the hilltop. You're an esteemed landowner in the place beyond pain or problems (Eph. 1:18-22). Think about it. If Christ is living in you, and if He is "above all rule and authority, power and dominion" (v. 21), are you dwelling in the basement or in the third-floor suite? It's so obvious—but often so overlooked. The enemy of your faith wants you to pack up your purpose and plans in a cardboard box and take them with you to the lower level.

Of course, Christ called you to walk humbly with Him. And of course, self-denial is a key to Kingdom success. But you weren't born again to occupy a spiritual basement office. You were assigned to the third-floor suite: "God raised us up with Christ and seated us with him in the heavenly realms in Christ Jesus" (Eph. 2:6). You weren't called to cower like a mouse at a cat show! You were called to be a vessel filled by the Holy Spirit with heaven's courage.

What does all of that have to do with leading people? Everything! Every Christian leader must understand that he or she is not leading from a weakened position. Now, that's no reason to act haughty, aloof, or arrogant (1 Pet. 2:16-17). On the contrary, it's a reason to exude a Spirit-controlled confidence that comes from your position in Christ. Before you ever walk through the door of that potentially troubling business meeting, before you're forced to greet that carnal board chairman who has the attitude of Hitler's hair stylist, before you ever sit down and try to put the pieces of your ministry back together after a devastating tragedy—before anything else, you've already been declared a victor!

B. Focus on your affections. "Set your hearts on things above" (Col. 3:1). It's too easy to allow the things of earth to creep into our heavenly mission. Because of our relation to Adam, there's still a lot of earthly dust on our shoes! (Gen. 2:7). So Christian leaders are always encouraged to keep their shoes cleaned and polished to reflect the gleam of heaven.

Nothing *here* is worth more than anything there.

The desire to seek after earthly possessions or ecclesiastical positions will always try to surface and take prominence. But ultimately they will only add to the climate of adversity (around you and within you), not help you rise above it. If Christ and the Kingdom are first, Jesus promises, everything else will fall into place (Matt. 6:33).

C. Focus on your commission. "Set your minds on things above" (Col. 3:2). You were called to the greatest work: the seeking and saving of the lost and the education and encouragement of the saved. The things of time will always fight for your attention over the things of eternity. Plans, programs, and properties will always seek to dominate your thoughts. It will be your task to think of them only as a means to an end—not as ends in themselves.

You'll remember that Paul focused on the "prize," not the

"plans." The plans were simply stepping-stones toward the prize of the "high calling." Every Christian leader will need to decide whether or not his or her *actions* reflect his or her *mission*.

Besides, if you focus on establishing earthly thrones and dominions, all you can expect is earthly help. But if you focus on building the kingdom of Christ, you can expect the troops and treasures of heaven to be at your disposal!

D. Focus on your submission. "You died, and your life is now hidden with Christ in God" (Col. 3:3). Adversity is a tool that a sovereign God uses to fine-tune your personal faith and corporate ministry. It does not master you. You died to it when you were resurrected in Christ.

When you decided to lay down your fishing net—as did Christ's disciples—and pick up your cross, you made a conscious decision to share its cause and its consequence. And if you'll remember, the weather wasn't that sunny around the Cross! Why should we be surprised when adversity accompanies our cross-carrying?

But Jesus' cross is a symbol of victory over adversity. He taught us that. By submitting fully to His Heavenly Father's will, He accomplished His mission. And the worker benefits that we enjoy, including an eternal retirement plan, came out of the process.

Christ's suffering ultimately resulted in healing.

His death ultimately brought life.

His shame ultimately brought affirmation.

E. Focus on your vindication. "When Christ, who is your life, appears, then you also will appear with him in glory" (Col. 3:4). In one glorious moment of time—nearer now than ever—the Master will vindicate every wrong against His servants. The presence that is often hidden now will be fully revealed then! We sing, "He is here, hallelujah," and we know that deep in our spirit. But often our humanity clouds His proximity. Often we feel lonely and alone—about as popular as an acid rock band at a revival meeting.

But living above adversity calls for focusing on the final outcome. The New Testament writer to the Hebrew Christians penned a great reminder under the authority and inspiration of the Holy Spirit: "God is not unjust; he will not forget your work and the love you have shown him as you have helped his people and continue to help them" (Heb. 6:10).

There will be a payday someday. God will settle the score for every wrong against those who love Him and against those whom He loves. The principalities and powers of earth should be put on alert: *You can't mess with God's kids and get away with it!*

Christian leaders often take more beating than a badminton birdie. Some of the licks may be deserved, but more often they are undeserved. Living above the adversity means focusing on the final, God-planned vindication. Trying to get even simply wears you out as well as diverts you from your mission.

There's another important key to adjusting to adversity.

4. Keep an eye on the sky

The oversized vocalist of the feminine gender hasn't delivered her final rendition!

That's a very earthly way to try to convey a very important heavenly thought: *It's not over yet.* The last song hasn't been sung. Famed former baseball catcher and homespun philosopher Yogi Berra unwittingly put his slant on the truth of Scripture when he said, "It ain't over 'til it's over."

> For the creation was subjected to frustration, not by its own choice, but by the will of the one who subjected it, in hope that the creation itself will be liberated from its bondage to decay and brought into the glorious freedom of the children of God.
>
> We know that the whole creation has been groaning as in the pains of childbirth right up to the present time. Not only so, but we ourselves, who have the firstfruits of the Spirit, groan inwardly as we wait eagerly for our adoption as sons, the redemption of our bodies. For in this hope we were saved. But hope that is seen is no hope at all. Who hopes for what he already has? But if we hope for what we do not yet have, we wait for it patiently (*Rom. 8:20-25*).

The Bible teaches us that even while we watch the awesome and awful events of the end times unfold, we should lift up our heads, for our redemption is drawing near. Twenty-first-century Christian leaders need a hand to the plow, but they also need an eye to the sky.

Sooner than we think, the trumpet of the Lord will sound, and time will be no more. Francis Schaeffer nobly asked, "How shall we then live?"

There are several things we should do in light of Christ's return:

A. Remember that God's plan is being carried out. "The creation itself will be liberated from its bondage to decay" (Rom. 8:21). What a loving God started in a rather small garden setting (Eden) He is now fulfilling on a huge playing field (these times). He promised redemption from the deadly effects of Adam and Eve's rebellion. And just as the finest pottery must go through the fury of the fire to make it whole, so the plan of God for ultimate wholeness and holiness will sometime involve adversaries and adversity.

Christian leaders must never forget that they are part of an ongoing process of healing, even when they're going through times of personal or corporate pain. And they also must not forget that heaven is primed and ready to proceed with the rescue.

Leader, keep your eye on the sky. And recruit as many "sky-watchers" as you possibly can. Teach your people that the answer is on the way—Christ is coming. And make every effort to proactively dispel the shadows in your church or organization.

- Preach and teach the Lord's return.
- Set a tone of hope in your organizational or worship meetings.
- Walk and talk like a person of hope.
- Give prominence to Scripture.
- Counsel people to trust the Lord in trying times.
- Pray positively in public and in private.
- Put an outreach plan in motion.

B. Be alert to people in pain. "The whole creation has been groaning as in the pains of childbirth right up to the present time" (Rom. 8:22). The process of God's sovereign and unfolding plan includes times of tears as well as triumph. People in your community will be crying. According to Isa. 61:1, the Messiah was sent to

- "Preach good news to the poor"
- "Bind up the brokenhearted"
- "Proclaim freedom for the captives and release from darkness for the prisoners"

Thus as His servants, the poor, the brokenhearted, and the prisoners are in our assignment area. We must stay alert for them. Go to them quickly. Love them sacrificially. And readily give them the confident promises of God's unchanging Word.

C. Rest in the unsearchable and the invisible. "We hope for what we do not yet have" (Rom. 8:25). While you cannot fully understand it, God's promises are being fleshed out even in the rubble of these times. Songwriter Lidie H. Edmunds wrote,

> *My faith has found a resting place—*
> *Not in device nor creed:*
> *I trust the Ever-living One—*
> *His wounds for me shall plead.*

There's an unseen hand holding your hand. There's a company of unseen angels surrounding your ministry area. There are unsearchable riches being mined right now to supply your needs.

The God of Matthew, Mark, Luke, and John is with you.

The Supplier for Paul, Silas, Timothy, and Barnabas is meeting your need.

The wisdom that flowed through Priscilla and Aquila is yours for the asking.

The Energizer of James and Peter is your portion.

New Testament leaders had no greater source than yours. You have planted your feet on the ground that does not shake against the attacks of 10,000 enemies.

You have tapped the wellspring of forgiveness and eternal life.

You have offered up what you cannot possibly keep for the very things that you cannot possibly lose.

March on with confidence.

Preach with power.

Plan with hope.

Lead with authority.

Pray with diligence.

And keep an eye on the sky!

Notes

Introduction

1. Michael Ross, "Changing Role of Religious Leadership," *Indianapolis Star,* 4 October 1998, D3.

2 Leith Anderson, *Leadership That Works: Hope and Direction for Church and Parachurch Leaders in Today's Complex World* (Minneapolis: Bethany House Publishers, 1999), 26.

Chapter 1

1. Hudson T. Armerding, *Leadership* (Wheaton, Ill.: Tyndale House Publishers, 1978), 26.

2. Bruce B. Auster, "A Legend on Ice," *U.S. News and World Report,* 6 December 1999, 22.

3. James C. Humes, *Churchill: Speaker of the Century* (New York: Stein and Day), 291.

4. Madeleine L'Engle, *Walking on Water: Reflections on Faith and Art,* quoted in "How Jesus Defines Success," PreachingToday.com, 20 February 2000, 1.

5. Anderson, *Leadership That Works,* 44.

6. Paul Davidson, "Hackers Join the Other Side," *USA Today,* 6 January 2000, A1.

7. Source unknown.

8. Jay C. Grelen (Oct. 25, 1998), "Why Everyone Looks Up to David Robinson" <www.christianity.net/cr/8R2/8R2020.html>.

9. Anderson, *Leadership That Works,* 68.

Chapter 2

1. Fred Smith Sr., *Leading with Integrity,* ed. David L. Goetz (Minneapolis: Bethany House, 1999), 13.

2. Ibid., 24.

3. *Merriam-Webster's Collegiate Dictionary,* 10th ed., s.v. "integrity."

4. John C. Maxwell, *The 21 Irrefutable Laws of Leadership: Follow Them and People Will Follow You* (Nashville: Thomas Nelson, 1999), 4.

5. Maxie Dunnam, "What Will Remain After You're Gone?" in *Leading with Vision,* ed. Dale Galloway (Kansas City: Beacon Hill Press of Kansas City, 1999), 153.

6. Max Lucado, *Grace for the Moment: Inspirational Thoughts for Each Day of the Year,* ed. Terri Gibbs (Nashville: J. Countryman, 2000), 252.

7. Keith Drury, "The Bigger They Are, the Harder They Fall" <www.indwes.edu/Tuesday>.

8. Elmer Towns, "Visionary Leaders Encounter Greatness," in Galloway, *Leading with Vision,* 136.

9. Tim Bowman, "What's a 'Significant' Ministry?" *Leadership Journal* 20, no. 3 (summer 1999): 99.

10. James Earl Massey, "Developing a Visionary Church That Has Integrity," in Galloway, *Leading with Vision,* 27.

11. "Six Pillars of Character," *NRB,* November 1999, 28.

12. Leighton Ford, *Transforming Leadership: Jesus' Way of Creating Vision, Shaping Values and Empowering Change* (Downers Grove, Ill.: InterVarsity Press, 1991), 84.

13. George H. W. Bush, quoted in *Leadership: A Treasury of Great Quotations for Those Who Aspire to Lead,* ed. William Safire, Leonard Safire (New York: Simon and Schuster, 1990), 22.

14. Paul Lee Tan, *Encyclopedia of 7700 Illustrations* (Rockville, Md.: Assurance Publishers, 1979), n.p.

Chapter 3

1. Denny Gunderson, *The Leadership Paradox* (Seattle: YWAM Publishing, 1997), 109.

2. Ibid.

3. Mary Kay Ash, quoted in *Leadership,* 168.

4. Ford, *Transforming Leadership,* 210.

5. Ibid.

6. *Merriam-Webster's Collegiate Dictionary,* 10th ed., s.v. "benchmark."

7. Rick Reilly, "Life of Reilly," *Sports Illustrated,* 21 August 2001, 103, at <sportsillustrated.cnn.com/inside_game/magazine/life_of_reilly>.

8. <www.gospelcom.net/ifc/ifc68/ifc68pg5.shtiml>.

9. Tom Erlich, "Real Authority Starts with Good Listening," *Indianapolis Star,* 29 January 2000, G2.

Chapter 4

1. Brian D. Molitor, *The Power of Agreement* (Nashville: Broadman and Holman, 1999), quoted at <www.crosswalk.com> Live It Channel.

2. Mark A. Smith and Larry M. Lindsay, *Leading Change in Your World* (Marion, Ind.: Triangle Publishing, 2001), 76.

3. Molitor, *The Power of Agreement,* quoted at <www.crosswalk.com> Live It Channel.

4. Personal interview, January 1, 2000.

5. George Barna, *User Friendly Churches* (Ventura, Calif.: Regal Books, 1991), 144.

6. George Barna, *Boiling Point, It Only Takes One Degree: Monitoring Cultural Shifts in the 21st Century* (Ventura, Calif.: Regal Books, 2001), 246.

7. Gary McIntosh, *The McIntosh Church Growth Network: Ministry Insights for Church Leaders* 11, July 1999, 1.

8. Misael Zaragoza, "Looking for High-Potential Leaders," 18 December 2000, at <www.inspiredchristian.org/cyber/121800mz.html>.

9. Cathie Cowie, "Workplace in the Near Future," <www.crosswalk.com> 29 August 2001, 1.

10. Quoted in John R. Throop, "Max DePree on Leadership, Life and Sacred Trust: Leading from the Chair," *Christian Management Report,* January-February 1999, 7.

11. Nelson Searcy, Jimmy Britt, and Kwan Ihn, *The SmartLeaders Edge,* August 2001, at <www.smartleadership.com>.

12. McIntosh, *The McIntosh Church Growth Network: Ministry Insights for Church Leaders* 11, October 1999, 1.

13. Barna, *Boiling Point,* 240.

Chapter 5

1. *Merriam-Webster's Collegiate Dictionary,* 10th ed., s.v. "energy."

2. Gary Fenton, *Your Ministry's Next Chapter: The Best Is Yet to Come,* ed. David L. Goetz (Minneapolis: Bethany House, 1999), 52, 58.

3. Quoted in *Leadership,* 22.

4. Elmer Towns, "Visionary Leaders Encounter Greatness," in Galloway, *Leading with Vision,* 128.

5. Anderson, *Leadership That Works,* 120.

6. E. Glenn Wagner, *Escape from Church, Inc.: The Return of the Pastor-Shepherd* (Grand Rapids: Zondervan, 1999), quoted in *Current Thoughts and Trends,* April 2000, 19.

7. Smith, *Leading with Integrity,* 95.

8. Keith Naughton, "Tired of Smile-Free Service?" *Newsweek,* 6 March 2000, 44.

9. Armerding, *Leadership,* 69.

10. Smith and Lindsay, *Leading Change in Your World,* 114.

11. Thom S. Rainer, *Surprising Insights from the Unchurched and Proven Ways to Reach Them* (Grand Rapids: Zondervan, 2001), 198.

12. David J. Spittal, "A Legacy of Spiritual Leadership," *Light from the Word,* November 14, 1998 (devotional).

13. Bruce Wilkinson, *Secrets of the Vine* (Sisters, Oreg.: Multnomah Publishers, 2001), 39.

Chapter 6

1. Harlan Cleveland, quoted in *Leadership,* 23.

2. *Merriam-Webster's Collegiate Dictionary,* 10th ed., s.v. "jibe."

3. Larry W. Osborne, "Making Changes Without Getting People Steamed," *Leadership* <www.christianity.net/leadership/8L2/8L2042.html>, 25 October 1998, 1.

4. Quoted in Dick Wynn, "Leadership Is a Fine Art," *Emerging Young Leaders* newsletter, winter 1999—2000, 1.

5. Joseph D. Allison, "Management: The Art of Handling the Unusual," *Evangel Press Newsletter,* winter 1999—2000, 2.

6. Ben Patterson, "God Loves the Little Things, the Secret Things His Servants Do," *Leadership* (fall 1996). 25 October 1996,
<www.christianity.net/leadership/6L4130.html>.

7. Jeren Rowell, "Future Church: Connections," *The Communicator,* Nazarene Publishing House, vol. 13, no. 16 (September 2000), 1.